SARAH GRIFFIT

BLESSED MINDS

BREAKING THE SILENCE ABOUT
NEURODIVERSITY

chalice
PRESS

Haikus that appear in the book (except for haikus in chapters 3, 4, and 9 written by the author) are used by permission and are from The Journal of Learning Development in Higher Education ISSN: 1759-667X Special Issue 29: ALDinHE Conference Collaborative Proceedings October 2023. Increasing neurodiversity awareness through a community of practice, by Karen Welton of Arts University Plymouth, UK and Jennie Dettmer University of Hertfordshire, UK

Print: 9780827203440

EPUB: 9780827203457

EPDF: 9780827203464

ChalicePress.com

I am so grateful and delighted for this sacred work. Spirituality is so much deeper than cognitive style, and we tragically limit and minimize people by rating and ranking them based upon their cognitive signature. Spiritual knowing is all of ours, nobody is left out. We are built to share through our awakened hearts a love that runs deeper than our mind's calculations, intellect, cognition, or 'downstream' discernment, as it is our participation in the ultimate, sacred transcendent relationship. G-d's love, through us as carriers, fluidly flows between all people. Heartful spiritual contact reaches right through the broad range of cognitive styles with which we have been endowed. Sarah Griffith Lund reminds us to tune into the awakened heart of every person whose deeper presence awaits our sacred touch.

> — Lisa Miller, Ph.D, *New York Times* bestselling author and award-winning researcher at Columbia University

In *Blessed Minds*, Sarah Griffith Lund weaves her personal story, pastoral experience, and information about neurodiversity into a tapestry that is brightly colored by stories from congregations who are intentionally including and celebrating the lives and gifts of people with various forms of neurodiversity, including those who feel called to ministry themselves. Using a strategy she names in the book as important for fostering inclusion, she invites readers to play with multiple implications of affirming neurodiversity as part of God's diverse and beloved creation while also providing clear, flexible and helpful guidelines for celebrating that diversity within the lives of individual congregations. It's engaging *and* fun to read!

> — Bill Gaventa, author, speaker, trainer, and consultant in faith and disability, founder and Director Emeritus of the Institute of Theology and Disability and initial President of the Disability Ministry Network

In this fifth installment of Sarah Griffith Lund's "Blessed" series, she once again opens our eyes to see the blessedness of all God's children, some of whom are often forgotten. This time, with her focus on neurodiversity, she shows how our minds are a blessing even though one may differ from what is considered typical. Not only does she invite us to see with new eyes, but she also challenges faith communities to put out a welcome mat for the neurodiversity present in Christ's church. Through stories of people who are neurodiverse and stories of faith communities actively providing a welcoming atmosphere for neurodiversity, Lund offers insights and practical ways for individuals and faith communities to do so as well. This is an important book to help members of faith communities, both lay and clergy alike, recognize and honor the lives, spirituality, and blessedness of all God's neurodiverse children.

> — Rev. Dr. Hollie M. Holt-Woehl, Luther Seminary and St. John's School of Theology-and Seminary

Blessed Minds is a must-have book on why and how to embrace neurodiversity in the church. Sarah Griffith Lund offers a theological and practical guide to confronting ableism and building a neuroinclusive church at the intersections. She calls us to listen to neurodivergent parables and pray neurodivergent prayers. This book is an invaluable resource that is accessible and enjoyable to read.

> — Rudolph P. Reyes II, Assistant Professor of Christian Ethics and Latinx Studies, Garrett-Evangelical Theological Seminary

Blessed Minds is a transformative call to embrace neurodiversity as a vital expression of God's creation. Sarah Griffith Lund offers profound theological insights alongside personal narrative, challenging stigma and inspiring a vision of a truly inclusive church. With courage and compassion, this book invites us to celebrate the unique gifts of neurodivergent individuals and to build communities where all minds are honoured as blessed. Essential reading for anyone committed to justice, belonging, and the flourishing of all God's children.

> — Rev. Professor John Swinton, King's College University of Aberdeen, School of Divinity, History and Philosophy

Judaism exhorts people to utter blessings upon encountering aspects of our world. One of my favorites is the blessing to be recited upon observing a human or animal perceived as different.

> — Baruch Atah Adonai, Eloheinu Melech Haolam, m'shaneh habriyot Blessed are You, Adonai our God, Ruler of the Universe, who makes people different

Part of Adonai's nature, something that is to be praised, is their creation of diversity. Upholding diversity can be a challenge, but it is a divine directive. All people are created in God's image, and just as God contains multitudes, so does humanity. Lund masterfully speaks alongside other neurodiverse folks, past, present, and future to encourage and equip the church to not only embrace such multitudes of difference but to celebrate them.

Blessed Minds is an invitation to a celebration, a celebration of God's goodness in creating diversity where all people are invited as our true selves, in all our messy glory. This book helps us to imagine this celebration. It is a one with stimming and shouting and singing and sobbing, where shame is pushed aside, and stories are shared. It is my sincere hope that Lund's invitation is heard, accepted, and extended.

> — Dr. Kirsty Jones, Ashland University, Religion Department

Dedicated to my mother, Jennie Murrell Griffith, in celebration of her over four decades of service in early childhood public education, where she created learning environments for the flourishing of all blessed minds.

"I do not believe the fact that I am Autistic is an offense to God. I do not believe I should seek to be anything other than human. This is who I am and how God created me."

—Lamar Hardwick, Autistic Pastor

"Collectively, through our stories, our connections, and our actions, disabled people will continue to confront and transform the status quo. It's who we are."

—Alice Wong, Founder and Director of the Disability Visibility Project

Contents

Foreword

The concept of neurodiversity is not new, but it is increasingly receiving greater attention as people come to view their own experiences from this perspective. On social media, for example, you're bound to find people reflecting on their experiences or diagnoses in light of neurodiversity. While the idea of neurodiversity has gained more recognition in recent years, few resources explore the insights of the neurodiversity paradigm for the purpose of faith formation and ministry. What can the church learn from the neurodiversity movement, and how can the vision of neurodiversity in God's good creation deepen our relationship with God and strengthen our care for others?

I'm excited to say that the book you're holding helps us answer these important questions.

Emerging from the Autism rights movement, the concept of neurodiversity has traditionally been focused on the lived experiences of Autistic people. It sprang up as a rallying cry, asserting Autism is not a condition that needs to be cured but instead a way of being in the world that should be accepted and celebrated. In short, neurodiversity emphasizes the natural variation in the way people think, learn, and live in the world. Since the beginning of the movement, the term "neurodiversity" has been a bit of a moving target. People use the term in different ways in different areas of life. Ultimately, the gift of the neurodiversity paradigm is that it expands our understanding and imagination of the world.

In recent years, the conversation around the neurodiversity paradigm has expanded to include a broader range of mental, emotional, and behavioral differences. The concept of "neurodivergence" has become a kind of umbrella term, under which many conditions and diagnoses fall. To be "neurodivergent" simply means "having a mind that functions in ways which diverge significantly from the dominant societal standards of 'normal.'"[1] While the neurodiversity paradigm vehemently rejects the pathologizing of forms of neurodivergence that are innate aspects of a person's being in the world, such as Autism, it also recognizes there are some forms of neurodivergence that are undesirable for individuals, such as certain mental health challenges. While many people with conditions

---

[1] Nick Walker, *Neuroqueer Heresies: Notes on the Neurodiversity Paradigm, Autistic Empowerment, and Postnormal Possibilities* (Fort Worth: Autonomous Press, 2021), 38.

like bipolar disorder or depression see themselves as neurodivergent, they do not celebrate their diagnoses. What is important here is that we listen to how people understand and reflect on their own experiences. Sarah Griffith Lund's expansive vision of neurodiversity, one that can include both desirable and undesirable experiences of neurodivergence, helps us do just that.

What Lund shows throughout this book is how people of faith can take up the perspective of neurodiversity and the concept of neurodivergence to understand the body of Christ in new and exciting ways. Lund is well positioned to write this book. She has firsthand experience, pastoral sensitivity, and a practical theological vision. It's important to note Lund's work is aimed at a particular problem: what scholars in the emerging field of neurodiversity studies call "neuronormativity." This has to do with the barriers established when perspectives and experiences of neurotypical people—those traditionally regarded as "normal"—are placed at the center of the community. This is why *Blessed Minds* is so vital. Lund does not just teach the church about the neurodiversity paradigm or the history of the neurodiversity movement. She is *teaching for faith formation* within the context of congregational ministry and in light of the fact of neurodiversity. Lund's vision is expansive. And what she's focused on is a particular posture that the church can take—a posture oriented toward justice.

Don't just read this book. Put it into practice. As you read, ask how you might create worship experiences that honor different sensory needs and processing styles. How might you adapt education programs to serve learners of all neurotypes? How might you transform your understanding of spiritual gifts and calling to recognize the unique contributions of all people? Use the resources in each chapter to consider what the neurodiversity paradigm might teach us about prayer, worship, and community. But before you continue reading, pause and ask God to bring to life for you this vision of God's neurodiverse creation.

Michael Paul Cartledge

Princeton, New Jersey

Welcome and Announcements

Welcome to *Blessed Minds: Breaking the Silence About Neurodiversity.* Please make yourself comfortable as we engage in this exploration of neurodiversity and spirituality together. No matter who you are or where you are on the neurodivergent journey, I am glad you are here. This book is written from my perspective as a person of faith who strives for justice for all, including folks who experience oppression and discrimination of any kind. My views reflect my beliefs and values of equality for LGBTQ+, Black, Indigenous, Hispanic, Asian, and other people of color, disabled folks, and anyone who feels their life is not valued or celebrated by the church and society.

A couple of brief "announcements" about this book. The neurodiversity movement is indebted to the Autism community, Autism self-advocates, and neurodiversity activists, without whom the idea for *Blessed Minds* would not have been possible. It has taken decades of advocacy for neurological differences to be included within the broader categories of human diversity. For centuries neurodiversity was associated with deviance, disorder, and, in religious communities, theological concepts of sin. It's time for the church to stop traumatizing and spiritually harming people's bodyminds in the name of God.

This book expands the boundaries and understanding of neurodiversity based on theological concepts of God's unlimited, borderless, and unconditional love. Some readers may be uncomfortable with how expansively and inclusively this book explores neurodiversity as a spiritual movement. For undoubtedly this book challenges past and even current ways of thinking about mental health experiences, disability, and neurodiversity. It ponders where mental health realities might belong within the neurodiversity spiritual movement.

Moreover, this book shares stories about the origin of the neurodiversity movement, and not everyone agrees about how it all got started. The neurodiversity community is not stagnant nor monolithic. It is dynamic, ever-changing, and constantly evolving: movements move. Not everyone thinks the same way, believes the same thing, or has the same faith or beliefs or values. What a boring world it would be if we did! This is especially true in the neurodiversity movement. The information I have collected for this book contains stories about people whose views I do not always agree with, but I include their stories here because they are part of the larger unfolding, sometimes messy story. Important questions to keep in mind as you read this book: How does the story of neurodiversity get told? Whose voices are amplified, and whose voices are silenced? Part of breaking the silence means listening to the stories that have been forced underground.

I invite you to be open to this ongoing, expansive exploration of neurodiversity and what it means for people of faith. If something is uncomfortable for you, take a break, journal about your thoughts and feelings, and do something that feels good for your bodymind. Engage with this material in a way that is a blessing for you. Thank you for believing in our collective power to create a more loving, inclusive world for all blessed minds.

As a person of faith, I believe the neurodiversity movement is necessary to combat the stigma and shame that undermines the well-being of neurodivergent folks. Thanks to collective hard work in the secular fields of disability and neurodiversity studies, we in spiritual and religious communities can continue creating a neurodiversity movement that includes faith communities. This book invites us all to consider how the expansiveness of God's love removes barriers to inclusion and calls us to make space for people with diverse mental health realities and disabilities within the neurodiversity movement.

Each of the following chapters begins with a haiku written by a neurodivergent person, followed by a faith-inspired parable created to help to honor the power of blessed minds throughout this book. These parables are inspired by stories of Jesus in the Bible. In writing these neurodivergent parables, I wondered what it would look like for us to have sacred stories explicitly about neurodiversity in the Bible. I also wondered what might have happened "behind the scenes" in the biblical stories, things that were not written down. I hope these imaginative parables help open your mind to ways our own sacred stories might give witness and testify to the power of spirituality in the neurodiversity movement.

At the beginning of each chapter you will find a highlighted listing of key words from the chapter that I hope will assist in understanding. Besides that, most of the chapters end with a story illustration and a reflection question. Engage the parts of this book that are helpful to you, and be open to God's creative and playful Spirit as we imagine how faith can shape our understanding of the neurodiversity movement that includes mental health realities.

There are symbols to help mark sections of the book: haiku (heart), key word (key), prayer (dove), story illustration (infinity), and reflection question(question mark). There is a glossary in the back that collects all the key words from the book.

This is a book you can read quietly or out loud, alone or with your dog or cat or bird or turtle, with a friend or a group. Adapt this book! You are invited to dream and expand, to take up space and to be more fully who God is calling you to be and become. I hope this book helps you feel less alone. I hope this book helps you feel loved.

Creating this book helped me accept my own mind as blessed, and this comforts me, especially when I feel worried something is "wrong" with the way my brain works. Rather than self-stigma and shame, I am coming to a place of acceptance and even joy. I smile in my spirit and say "that's just how my brain works." I ask for the support and accommodations I need, such as different overhead lighting or further conversation to help me better understand something that confuses me. The neurodiversity paradigm has positively transformed the way I think about myself and how I interact with others. I hope this book inspires you to embrace your bodymind as blessed: God loves all of you, right now, just as you are. I hope this book helps us all love one another and honor the beautiful array of diversity we each bring into the world.

When I saw that my local public library had the book *Neurodiversity for Dummies*,[1] I took it as a sign from the universe confirming the time has come to create a new book—one I might have titled *Neurodiversity for the Church*. This book is also a movement of God's Spirit, who is doing something new. Do you perceive it, too? God is inviting us to cast out the evil spirits of stigma and shame by breaking the silence and creating communities of belonging for people with neurological differences and mental health realities so that all minds shall be blessed.

Introduction

"There is always light, if only we are brave enough to see it—if only we are brave enough to be it." I love these words by Amanda Gorman, the youngest inaugural poet in U.S. history, because they represent the hope I carry within me as a person of faith. Psalm 23:4 declares, "Even though I walk through the valley of the shadow of death, I fear no evil." My hope comes from the light of God's love that guides me through and out of the valley of the shadows. When we are brave, we can see God's light. When we are brave, we can *be* a spark of God's light.

While researching at my local library for this project, I came across the young adult book *Rebel Girls Celebrate Neurodiversity: 25 Tales of Creative Thinkers.*[2] And guess who is the first celebrated neurodivergent rebel girl? Amanda Gorman. I had no idea she was neurodivergent. *Rebel Girls Celebrate Neurodiversity* tells the story of when Amanda was a little girl and diagnosed with an auditory processing disorder. Amanda could hear, but her brain had to work hard to make sense of sounds. Certain words and letters of the alphabet were hard for her to say. As a child, Amanda found solace in writing poems.

Like Amanda Gorman, as a child I also found comfort in writing poems because it enabled me to create an alternative world where I felt safe to share my thoughts and express my feelings. Later, I found ways to express my emotions through painting. The canvas became a mirror for my mind, colors and shapes expressing the feelings I did not have the words to describe. This is what I mean by the phrase "blessed minds."

Art, paintings, poetry—all come through blessed minds: minds blessed with abilities to create beauty, meaning, and human connections with the divine spark. Amanda Gorman's neurodivergence blessed the world when she recited her poem "The Hill We Climb" at the 2021 inauguration of President Joe Biden. I also appreciate the openness of President Biden about his own neurodivergence, his speech condition of stuttering.

Thanks to pioneers like Amanda Gorman, people today are more comfortable than ever before discussing matters of diversity and difference, mental health, and personal challenges. Too often, however, there is still stigma and shame when one's brain works in ways deemed too far outside of an arbitrary norm or when one's struggles make others uncomfortable. Sadly, while the church should be a place of unconditional acceptance, differences and symptoms originating in the brain sometimes prove particularly challenging for Christians to understand. The teenager who can't stay quiet and still in worship. The man whose comments in Bible study leave others scratching their heads. The woman who remains depressed, despite everything for which she can be grateful. Many faith communities count these folks among their members and friends yet keep them on the margins. People with brain differences experience discrimination even in the church. As people of faith, we can work together to help make faith communities places of belonging for all people, including people with mental health experiences, disabilities, and neurodiversity.

This book explores what it might mean for the church to honor the incredible diversity of our minds—*neuro*diversity. Our minds are part of our body, connected to our whole selves. Our mind and body are one. For the purpose of this conversation about neurodiversity, emphasis is placed on the brain or the mind because of its unique role in shaping our identities. Our bodyminds are united and diverse; this is to be celebrated. This book explores how the church can convey that our diversity is sacred, not shameful. It suggests how the church can bless the diversity of our minds as gifts from God. This book also claims that God's creation of neurodiversity is vast and, well, diverse! From a faith perspective, neurodiversity includes all forms of brain differences, including mental health realities.

In my professional role as a local church pastor serving in ordained ministry for over twenty years, and in my roles as family member and friend, I use the following affirmations often because I know they are true. I place them here as a resource for you to use as a blessing. If you experience stigma and shame related to the way your brain works, know that:

You are holy and whole.

Your mind is sacred.

Your body is sacred.

Your spirit is sacred.

There is nothing shameful about your brain and how it works.

Your mind is blessed.

Your bodymind is blessed.

We all have blessed minds!

If you do not yourself experience such stigma related to brain differences or neurodiversity, but aspire to support others in your community who do, consider learning and internalizing these affirmations anyway. Share them with others as part of your spiritual practice.

There is debate surrounding who gets credited for coining the word "neurodiversity." As with many emerging concepts, multiple folks sometimes manifest new ideas around the same time. Academic research into the origin story confirms the term "neurodiversity" was the collective result of conversations online. Autistic academics confirm that "the history of neurodiversity is sometimes difficult to pin down because it is not especially well documented. A lot of organizing occurred on the early Internet, in now-defunct listservs, message boards and blogs. Much has been lost."[3] Although the earliest conversations about neurodiversity are not documented, we honor and celebrate the first pioneers of the neurodiversity movement, many of whose names we will never know.

Some say that Australian Jewish sociologist Judy Singer midwifed the concept of neurodiversity in 1998, the same year Google was invented. Singer is the daughter of a Holocaust survivor. She discovered in her forties that her mother was not only greatly affected by past trauma but was also Autistic. Around the same time, Judy learned she and her own daughter were likewise Autistic. Though a clinical definition of Autism did exist back in the 1950s, having a mother with Autism was not talked about.

In a 2023 interview for *The Guardian*[4] as an adult reflecting on her mother's mental struggles and her own, Singer noticed that the two of their minds seemed to work differently than those of other people. Studying humans in the context of all living things, Singer noticed that biological diversity was not only necessary for a healthy environment, but a gift. Ecological systems thrive in diversity: think about the Monteverde rainforest in Costa Rica or the Alaskan wilderness. Biodiversity is the gift of God's good creation, and human neurodiversity is no different. All our brains are created good as part of God's good creation.

Autism was originally thought of as a disease in need of a cure. The puzzle piece logo used for many years conveyed the idea of Autistic individuals as an enigma or a mystery to be solved. Today the puzzle piece logo is problematic for several reasons, including:[5]

1. It implied that Autistic people were incomplete or needed to be "solved."

2. The childlike, primary colors often used suggested that Autism only affects children.

3. It perpetuated the idea of Autism as a problem rather than as a different way of experiencing the world.

Autism advocates have since helped to situate Autism as part of the full continuum of the ways our brains work—the spectrum of neurodiversity. The symbols tell the story of the evolving understanding, from the puzzle piece to more inclusive symbols like the infinity loop, reflecting a broader change in how we approach neurodiversity.

Neurodiversity has its own symbol: a rainbow infinity loop. I love this image: the rainbow, which reminds Christians of God's promise to sustain creation, plus the infinity sign, which suggests the never-ending possibilities of our human imaginations. In the rainbow of diversity, I imagine there is a place for all types of brains within the color continuum. The rainbow of neurodiversity celebrates all brains as equal and included as part of God's good creation. All brains are created equal in the rainbow of God's love.

The Religious Roots of the Neurodiversity Movement

In the book *NeuroTribes*,[6] author Steve Silberman recalls Judy Singer's story about growing up Jewish and attending synagogue with her family. The rabbi once gave her a "thought-provoking assignment" to reimagine the Ten Commandments for modern times and "make them better than God's." This assignment may sound shocking and disrespectful to some people because it sounds like we are being asked to "play God." However, this intellectual exercise was a way to deeply engage teachings of the faith tradition. Reflecting Singer's deep commitment to the well-being of the environment, she created the first commandment: "Honor diversity, lest thou endeth up like unto the cactus of the desert." I wonder what she meant by her reference to a cactus. I've spent time on retreat praying in the desert, walking among the cacti, and found them delightful companions for spiritual contemplation. Perhaps she imagined cacti as symbols of being alone, isolated, and prickly because of not honoring diversity.

This story illustrates the spiritual value of honoring all of creation as a core value embedded in one of the beginning concepts of neurodiversity. I imagine the role of faith in this origin story of the word "neurodiversity," a story that sprang from a sacred conversation Singer had when her rabbi challenged her to think of a "better" list of ten commandments than those Moses received from God on Mount Sinai. Judy's neurodivergent brain, shaped by religious teachings and sacred text, took this opportunity to honor the diversity of God's creation of humankind. I thank God for the gift to imagine a world in which God prioritizes honoring diversity.

Inspired by the rabbi's intellectual exercise for the purpose of growth and deepening of our faith, if I challenged you to create ten new commandments, what would you include in your list? Someone in my household might say, "Thou shall not steal my electronic device charging cable." Singer created this one: "Honor diversity." What if "honor diversity" were not simply a suggestion or a company marketing slogan but instead an actual commandment? How can we better honor diversity within the human family, and specifically diversity of the human mind?

Jesus valued diversity before it was a popular thing to do. Jesus taught throughout his ministry that we are beloved by God, no matter how rich or poor we are. He said that young people and elders alike are children of God, worthy of love. People of faith today can also believe that:

Jesus loves people whose brains are complex and different.

Jesus loves people who experience depression and anxiety.

Jesus loves people diagnosed with bipolar disorder.

Jesus loves people with suicidality.

Jesus loves Autistic people.

Jesus loves ADHDers.

Jesus loves people who are dyslexic.

Jesus loves people who are in supportive therapy.

Jesus loves people fidgeting in the pews.

Jesus loves people who are neurodivergent.

Jesus loves all of us, no matter who we are or where we are in the rainbow of neurodiversity. Jesus loves your brain, we know, for the Bible tells us so.

***

By the time you finish reading this book and discussing it with others, I hope you can make all the above proclamations with joy and confidence.

What would it look like for followers of the Jesus Way, for disciples of Christ today, to honor diversity when it comes to brain functioning and mental health? What would it look like for your church to be a stigma-free zone when it comes to children, teens, young adults, and people of all ages who have neurodevelopmental differences and experience mental health symptoms? What would it look like for the church to embrace neuroinclusive ministries and celebrate ministers who are neurodivergent?

Is the church a safe place when it comes to taking off the mask and letting your neurodiversity show?

Or do people in your church feel social pressure to mask and pass for "normal," whatever that is? In what ways?

I have multiple generations of neurodivergent people in my family. We are a neurofamily. Between my husband and me, in multiple generations of our families, we have bipolar disorder, depression, complex PTSD, anxiety, Autism, ADHD, stuttering, and addiction. I know what it is like to wear a mask to church and pretend everything is fine, covering up my own difficulties, differences, and pain to appear normal—whatever "normal" is supposed to be. We mask all the time: at church, at school, at work, online, and at home. It's exhausting!

Over my lifetime I have perfected the art of masking. No wonder: I started masking when I was a little girl. My parents divorced, and I grew up lying to friends about who I am because I was so ashamed of my father's serious and chronic, untreated bipolar disorder. As a child, I had no understanding of the neurological root causes of his behaviors because no one had told me his brain was different and needed accommodations. My father faced significant barriers to getting mental health support, including self-stigma, and no matter how hard we tried he was not able to navigate his mental health differences with enough support. For our family, this meant that we experienced his harmful behaviors as part of his identity, instead of behaviors that could be managed. For example, I thought his mood swings, anger, and harmful behaviors were somehow my fault. From the time I was a young child, I was scared and confused. I was afraid that if my friends knew my dad was homeless, they wouldn't want to be my friends anymore. I kept quiet about the stress and chaos at home. I began to mask my own experiences of mental health symptoms. Sometimes we mask because we feel we have no choice. It's how we survive. I masked my own experiences of anxiety, self-harm, bedwetting, and dissociation caused by childhood trauma. I wanted to fit in with the other kids at school. I didn't want my friends to know I was different. According to Janae Elisabeth, researcher-storyteller and neurodiversity advocate: "Masking is a range of conscious to subconscious survival response. Sometimes it is more intentional. But mostly it's an automatic fawn response. In our childhood we build a persona that is normative enough that we do not get targeted as different."

It turns out masking is common in neurodivergent families like mine. Jenara Nerenberg talks about this in her book *Divergent Mind: Thriving in a World that Wasn't Designed for You*. She says,

> Masking refers to an unconscious or conscious effort to hide and cover one's own self from the world, as an attempt to accommodate others and coexist. Research and anecdotal evidence show that an extensive amount of masking and "passing" is going on among women and girls, primarily because of the way women are socialized. Girls and women have been taught from an early age to "blend in," according to researchers and the many women I interviewed for this book. Often, women hear the common refrain "Oh, she's just sensitive. That's how girls are." This is a sloppy, but widespread, oversight in our culture.[7]

I dream of a world in which we do not need to wear masks—because we are unashamed.

I dream of a world that honors diversity of the mind.

I dream of a world in which my father could have enjoyed a longer life as a neurodivergent person with quality, accessible, and affordable health care.

I dream of a world in which no one feels they need to wear a mask and cover up how truly unique and beautiful they are.

I dream of a world in which it is OK not to be OK, where it's OK not to be "normal," even in the church, *especially* in the church.

I dream of a world in which the neurodiversity movement embraces the power of faith communities to expand the boundaries of inclusion, making room for all of God's children.

I dream of a world in which mental health realities are destigmatized and considered part of the human experience.

I dream of a world in which mental health realities, symptoms, and diagnoses are fully celebrated as included in the rainbow spectrum of neurodiversity.

I dream of a world in which we share the love of Christ with people who are neurodivergent and their families.

The good news is that more and more people are dreaming of a world that celebrates neurodiversity! I invite you to join me in helping to build a more just world for all and to create communities that honor and celebrate neurodiversity. This is what it means to treat each other as sacred. This is what it means to celebrate our blessed minds.

For people of Christian faith, celebrating neurodiversity is what it means to be a Christian. Jesus' life, death, and resurrection show us the way to abundant life. Jesus said the greatest commandment of all is this: Love God with your whole heart and mind, and love your neighbor as yourself. This includes our neurodiverse neighbors and selves, too.

Church, of all places, is where human diversity should and can be honored, celebrated, and treated as sacred, for in diversity we see the divine. It is time to praise God for the glory of the neurodiversity of creation. It's time to create a neuroinclusive church.

May we all have the courage to follow the call of God's Spirit and help churches, other faith communities, and ministry settings become sacred places for God's neurodivergent people and their loved ones.

***

While I am always learning from the others in the ever expanding and changing neurodivergent community, I do not speak on anyone else's behalf. The views expressed in this book are mine. If you are neurodivergent and your opinions are different, that is totally valid. After all, a movement inspired by honoring diversity stays true to its origin story by making space for different voices, stories, and expressions of itself. You decide how you identify yourself, how you want to be treated, and how your story is used. Do not let anyone else silence you. I am breaking the silence here, but I need your help. Use your voice, use your stories, use your power, and join this movement of breaking the silence about neurodiversity. The neurodiversity movement needs all of us!

If you identify as neurotypical, having a brain without significant differences that impact your daily functioning, this is an invitation to take time to listen and to seek to understand as we all work together—in all our beautiful diversity—to grow in community and embrace one another as fellow children of God. After all, we can claim and be proud of the religious roots of the neurodiversity movement. It is time to embrace neurodiverse joy as a gift from God.

CHAPTER ONE

What Is Neurodiversity?

Terminology
Scared of using the wrong word
But trying matters

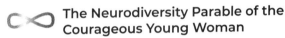 The Neurodiversity Parable of the Courageous Young Woman

After dinner, Jesus was walking along the shoreline of the Sea of Galilee when he heard a cry from inside a fishing boat that was tied to the shore. Jesus stopped walking in the sand and turned to look over at the boat. There, inside the boat, curled up in a fishing net, was a young woman crying.

Jesus walked over to her and said, "I heard your cry. What happened to you?"

Jesus sat down next to the boat and waited until the young woman stopped crying.

Then the young woman replied, "I don't know how to describe to you all that I am thinking, all that has happened to me, and all that I am feeling. I am overwhelmed and scared of using the wrong words. What if I mess up and say the wrong thing?"

Jesus said, "Do not be afraid. Take courage and speak from your heart. It is trying that matters."

Key Words in Chapter One

Disability: According to the United Nations Convention on the Rights of Persons with Disabilities, ratified by at least 182 countries around the world, disability "results from the interaction between persons with impairments and attitudinal and environmental barriers that hinders their full and effective participation in society on an equal basis with others."[8]

Mental health: The guiding source for all feelings, thoughts, behaviors, and social connections.

Mental health experiences: The unique mental health realities that can arise from within the brain or from external factors such as stigma, stress, and discrimination.

Mental illness: The interruption of feelings, thoughts, behaviors, and social connections.

Neurodivergent: Having a brain that functions differently from the majority of people.

Neurodiversity: The range of differences in brain function and behavior among all humans.

Neurospicy: A state of being that feels different for each person. As one friend explained it in a text to me, "When my brain is having a hard time processing different things and I am having a hard time with executive functioning skills, I feel all over the place or a hot mess." For some people, self-identifying as neurospicy can also be a form of playfulness.

Stimming: A form of self-stimulating behavior like arm or hand-flapping, finger-flicking, rocking, jumping, spinning, twirling, or body movements.

***

What Is Neurodiversity?

The concept of neurodiversity emerged from collective conversations. An international collection of Autism academics published a letter in April 2024 to help clarify the history of the neurodiversity movement. Here is an excerpt from their letter:[9]

> This letter discusses the origins of the concept and theory of neurodiversity. It is important to correctly attribute concept and theories to the people who developed them. For some time, the concept of neurodiversity has primarily been attributed to one person, Judy Singer. We consider the available evidence and show that the concept and theory in fact has multiple origins. We draw particular attention to recent archival findings that show the concept of "neurological diversity" was being used years earlier than previously thought. "Neurodiversity" means

the same thing as "neurological diversity" and does not change the theory in any way. We conclude that both the concept of neurological diversity or neurodiversity, and the body of theory surrounding it, should be understood as having been collectively developed by neurodivergent people.

What is helpful about this letter is the lesson learned that the neurodiversity movement is not only about one person's experience, faith, values, needs, ideas, or views, but more about how we come together respectfully to share with one another. We take our personal perspectives and bring them to community, honoring one another. That is what I am attempting to do here. I am sharing my story with you so that, together, we may find encouragement, support, guidance, and connection. My voice is only one voice. It's not the only voice or the most important voice. Your voice is important. Your experiences matter. We are not alone in this work. We each bring unique gifts to this collective work. I hope that we can together increase support for building up more inclusive, grace-filled and diverse communities of belonging for all God's people.

My exploration of neurodiversity has grown over the decade I've spent engaged in ministries of mental health and disability with faith communities across the United States. I have engaged in conversations with lay leaders and pastors in a range of contexts, from a rural church in Iowa to an inner-city church in Atlanta, from a coastal church in New England to a church in Palo Alto, to a mountain church in Colorado, and hundreds of churches in between. In each of these places and with each of these communities I have worked with leaders and laity to break the silence and end the stigma about disabilities and mental illness. These conversations began in response to my first book, *Blessed Are the Crazy: Breaking the Silence About Mental Illness, Family, and Church.*[10] They contained holy exchanges or stories about how mental health challenges alter our lives.

I received invitations from national organizations, such as the National Alliance on Mental Illness, to help educate people about the connection between faith and mental illness and its influence on families—specifically, on couples. That work inspired me to write my second book about marriage and mental illness, *Blessed Union: Breaking the Silence About Mental Illness and Marriage.*[11] I was then called by the national body of the United Church of Christ to serve on staff as its minister for disabilities and mental health justice. I accepted that role and also joined the national board of Mental Health America, the oldest mental health nonprofit in the United States.

In 2022 I published my third book *Blessed Youth: Breaking the Silence About Mental Illness with Children and Teens*,[12] as well as the companion book for youth, *Blessed Youth Survival Guide*.[13] These books are informed by my sixteen-year-old niece's suicide. Creating new resources was the best way I could think of to respond, as it helped me process my own grief while giving me hope that their messages might prevent a similar tragedy for another family.

Over the past decade as my life has evolved, so have the conversations about how we understand ourselves in relation to our brain chemistry and structure and the ways they affect our health, abilities, and relationships. As we continue to make new discoveries about the brain, we are continually adjusting the ways we think, understand, and talk about neurological functioning. Conversations are evolving about how we understand the interplay between our brains and spirituality. There remains much we do not yet understand about the way the brain works!

Because this book will use so many specialized concepts and terms, I begin with some definitions and introductions to these interconnected areas of study. As you journey with me through this book, we will consider how neurodiversity can be understood as inclusive of mental health realities and symptoms.

Mental Health, Mental Health Experiences, and Mental Illness

In my early work I chose to use the language of mental illness to highlight the more difficult aspects of mental health. Everyone has mental health, but not everyone has serious and chronic mental illness. Of all the definitions of mental health I have heard, the one that resonates the best with my experience is that of the World Health Organization:

> Mental health is a state of mental well-being that enables people to cope with the stresses of life, realize their abilities, learn well and work well, and contribute to their community. It is an integral component of health and well-being that underpins our individual and collective abilities to make decisions, build relationships and shape the world in which we live. Mental health is a basic human right. And it is crucial to personal, community, and socio-economic development.[14]

Moreover, mental health is not only a basic human right, but a God-given right. Our faith guides our understanding of what it means to advocate for mental health and disability rights for all people. We have a God-given right to flourish in our bodyminds.

In my family's experiences of mental health, we faced the realities of serious, chronic, and untreated mental health conditions and brain disorders. I felt God's call to break the silence about the hard stuff in my own life. My thought was that if I could share these stories, I might empower others to do likewise. I can't give others courage, but I can give them a vocabulary for stories they might want to share one day. I can do my part to help lead the way, in the hopes that others will also join the spiritual movement to break the silence to help end the stigma and shame.

Mental illness is language from the medical model that I found helpful for a time because it gave me permission to talk about the things that were painful, complicated, confusing, and harmful, especially in my own story. Our culture mostly accepts talk of physical illnesses caused by viruses and cancers and so on; if we want to discuss our brains, thoughts, or behaviors, using words like "illness" makes that easier to do. My father's bipolar disorder included symptoms that hurt him and his family. He had racing thoughts that caused him to harm us physically, he had delusions of being involved in international conspiracies to destroy our family, and he had thoughts of suicide. Using the language of mental illness created space for us to talk about the deep shadow sides of mental health, the far edges on the opposite side of the spectrum of mental wellness.

Though our language for the brain continues to evolve, I still believe it is important to honor the different ways people choose to talk about their personal experiences. The practice of breaking the silence and sharing our personal experiences with others is an important commitment and, at times, requires creativity in discussing neurodiversity. Some prefer the language of mental illness, some the language of "mental health challenges," and others the language of "mental health experiences." I like the way the phrase "mental health experiences" leaves room for fluctuation along the mental health spectrum from well to unwell. Especially when the brain is not chronically unwell, "mental health experiences" feels like a good fit because it honors the multitude of experiences and changing nature of mental health.

Mental illness is when the brain causes us to experience harmful symptoms that change and deplete our ability to live an abundant life. Just as we experience chronic illness in our bodies, we also experience illness in our minds. In breaking the silence about mental illness, it was important for me to tell stories the church had not invited us to share before because of the stigma and shame. Often, Christians have (and some Christians still do) viewed mental illness as resulting from sin, demon possession, a curse from God, or a lack of faith. It is time to bring the science of the biological, situational, and unknown causes of mental illness into the light to destigmatize mental illness in the church. There is no shame is experiencing mental illness.

Sharing stories about mental health experiences in church was healing for me because it allowed me to explore how God showed up during those difficult episodes of harm to offer grace, compassion, and love. Mental illness was not and is not God's punishment for sin. Mental illness was and is just part of the human condition. In the face of mental health experiences, God's role is to be compassionate and loving, not judgmental and withholding of grace.

Disability

Language like "illness" and "challenge" applies to physical as well as mental conditions, and often our physical health affects our mental health and vice versa. There is clear overlap. Having worked with both the United Church of Christ Disabilities Ministries and the United Church of Christ Mental Health Network, I realized some people's separation of physical and mental disabilities is an illusion. Both physical and mental disabilities are part of the larger spectrum of disabilities. The Americans with Disabilities Act of 1990 defines disability as a mental and/or physical impairment. Yet we persist in thinking of wheelchairs and not the experience of hearing voices as signs of disability. Churches are not legally bound to follow the ADA recommendations, so holding faith communities accountable requires ongoing advocacy, education, and support.

It is not the person but society that creates disability because of social structures that do not allow for accommodations that support full inclusion. Disability rights activism calls for equal rights, respect, and accessible environments in which all people can flourish. The church is called to embrace disability justice as a way to create communities of belonging for disabled people.

Honoring the connection between forces that affect both the brain and the whole body makes sense. In this way, brain disorders, challenges, and illnesses are part of physical disability, especially when they are chronic and get in the way of living an abundant life. Mental health symptoms are physical and are experienced throughout the body, such as migraines, digestive pain, nausea, just to name a few that I experience as physical symptoms of my complex post-traumatic stress disorder. Other forms of brain disabilities include intellectual and age-related brain disorders, such as dementia and Alzheimer's disease.

My oldest brother, Scott, helped me to understand the challenge of living with a mental disability by telling me the story about the time he applied for disability benefits. Scott was diagnosed with bipolar disorder in 1991, and after a decade Scott graduated in 2002 with a PhD. He was then hired by a university to be a professor. But in those first couple of years as a professor, his brain's ability to function became impaired in such a way that he could no longer perform his job to his employer's satisfaction. After he was fired, the staff person in the government office helping him with his disability paperwork looked at Scott and said: "When people look at me, they see my wheelchair and know that I am disabled. But when people look at you, they can't see your disability." Now in his fifties, my brother continues to be disabled from his bipolar disorder. He self-identifies as someone who lives with both a disability and a serious mental health diagnosis. He also says, "I am certainly neurodivergent."

Over the past decade of writing, teaching, listening, researching, and talking with others about mental illness, mental health challenges, mental health experiences, mental health symptoms, brain disorders, and disabilities, I continue to be open and curious about the various ways we interpret, understand, and express our stories. At the United Theological Seminary in Dayton, Ohio, I learned during my studies for a certificate program in disability ministry that what matters most in these conversations is being engaged with people who have firsthand knowledge and personal, lived experience.

A motto from the disability community rings true: "Nothing about us without us." As we talk about these complex issues, we will make mistakes with our language, we will make assumptions, and so long as we are committed to being in relationship with each other, we can be open to learning and growing. In the disability circles in which I move, mistakes are not only welcome but expected and encouraged. It's honorable to try, fail, and learn rather than never to try at all. Perfection is not the goal. People are more important than getting things perfect. This book is not perfect, even though I have tried my best. I ask forgiveness for the mistakes I have unknowingly made, and I hope to learn from them. I have found that there is humility and grace in the disability community that is seldom found elsewhere in society. The growing conversation around neurodiversity is one place where similar generosity could be found, especially with intentionality to extend grace as we navigate the expansiveness of the movement.

I invite you to extend grace as we engage in these conversations that attempt to expand our understanding of who is included in the neurodiversity movement. Is there room for people with chronic mental health symptoms, like my father and my brother? Is there room for people like me who have complex post-traumatic stress disorder? Is there room for my partner who has generalized anxiety disorder and depression? Can we create a broader definition of neurodiversity and grow the community to be a greater representation of diversity? Or are there limits to who is welcome in the neurodiversity movement? If so, what are they, and why? Who gets to decide who belongs and who doesn't belong? How might God be calling us to widen the welcome?

Neurodiversity, Neurodivergence, and Neurospicy

The prefix "neuro" comes from the Greek word *neuron*, which means nerve, sinew, or tendon. Our brains are a bundle of nerves, a physical network of electric impulses. "Diversity" comes from the Latin *diversitas*, which means a condition of being different. Therefore, "neurodiversity" is a word that encompasses the full spectrum of differences in the human brain, including those that might be identified as neurotypical and those considered neurodivergent. Distinctions between neurotypical and neurodivergent people are relatively arbitrary. When we talk about the mind, we remember we are bodyminds, connected as one whole body. There is no mind-body dualism or separation. Our body and mind are one, thus, the word "bodymind."

It is society that creates environments that are disabling to people whose bodies and brains are different. Likewise, being neurotypical is defined only by the lack of any recognized challenge or need for accommodation. Neurodiversity focuses on the benefits of brain differences, instead of identifying brain differences as inherently negative.

According to the Cleveland Clinic, neurodivergent is a "nonmedical term that describes people whose brains develop or work differently for some reason." In addition, the Cleveland Clinic reports, "experts' research also shows words and language related to neurodiversity make a difference in how people live. People who are neurodivergent and learn that it means they're different—not sick or defective—are more likely to be happier." The Cleveland Clinic includes in the category of neurodivergent people with "mental health conditions like bipolar disorder, obsessive-compulsive disorder and more."[15] Yet many people still do not consider mental health realities to be included in the neurodiversity movement. In this book, I encourage us to consider including mental health realities within the broad umbrella of neurodiversity.

To label oneself as neurodivergent means one intentionally includes oneself in the community of people whose brains are part of the diversity of human expression. More and more, the neurodiversity movement is growing because it is a grassroots movement in which more and more people are finding belonging, meaning, and support. To be neurodivergent is an identity that celebrates one's brain difference as contributing to humankind rather than being a deficit. There is power in self-identifying as neurodivergent because it offers a less stigmatized way to talk about the realities of brain differences.

Some neurodivergent folks embrace the word "neurospicy" as a way to describe the complexity, richness, and unique flavor of neurodiversity. As one friend put it, "Neurospicy is a particular way that I'm feeling in addition to being neurodivergent." Not everyone is a fan of this word, and that's OK. I appreciate the description of neurospicy provided by neurodivergent mental health care providers at NeuroSpark:[16]

> Neurospicy is obviously not a term you'll find in traditional or medical settings. It's a relatively new term and serves as a metaphorical construct that seeks to capture the vividness and intensity of our neurodivergent experiences and identities. Continuing with the metaphorical nature of the meaning of neurospicy, imagine your brain as a culinary concoction, where sensations, thoughts, and emotions blend together to create a symphony of flavors. Neurospicy represents the spicy, tangy, and savory aspects of the brain. Being neurospicy is about depth and complexity. In essence, neurospicy captures the extraordinary, intense, (and sometimes fierce!) aspects of neurodivergent personalities.

One way to envision how our understanding of the brain is evolving is to compare the brain to an ecosystem. In recent decades, scientists studying forest ecosystems have discovered that vast webs of fungi connect the root systems of trees under the ground, enabling plants to transfer water and important minerals like nitrogen and carbon to each other, as well as to warn each other of danger. Similarly, neuroscientists tell us the brain is connected to every other part of our body through a network of neurons. Thinking about it this way, then, perhaps the brain is more like a forest than a single tree or a single part of the body.

A healthy, vibrant forest supports many species and is beautiful in its diversity. If our individual bodies are like ecosystems and forests, then what happens when eight billion of us live together on the earth? What if humanity is like the ecosystem of a forest—the more diversity, the more beauty, and the more flourishing of abundant life?

God's Brainforest

Neurodiversity is connecting the dots between a healthy ecosystem of the human brain and the value of diversity for human flourishing. Today neurodiversity is a "big tent" word, and it seems to be getting bigger. The neurodiversity movement is growing. One place that prepares people for ministry under this big tent of neurodiversity is Princeton Theological Seminary's Institute for Youth Ministry. In the summer of 2022, Princeton launched an online course for youth ministry called "God's Brainforest."

"Brainforest" is a term that Thomas Armstrong, executive director of the American Institute for Learning and Human Development, coined to illustrate how the brain can be much more fully understood as a vibrant ecosystem than as a computer or machine. The brain is alive and always adapting to its environment and is organic in its response to change. The brain is not a broken machine that needs to be repaired. The brain is continually growing, dying, reforming, and transforming. This metaphor of the brain as brainforest goes beyond the binaries of broken/non-broken or sick/healthy or disabled/able-bodied or ill/well.

By no longer describing the brain as a machine, we can move away from the idea that there is one blueprint and universal instruction manual for the brain. Armstrong says, "By emphasizing the specialness of the child's brain, we can be more scientifically accurate than those who favor the broken brain hypothesis, and more importantly, we can support the child's or teen's dignity and integrity as a whole human being."[17] Under the big tent of neurodiversity, words like brainforest emerge, opening possibilities for our communities to adapt and change.

Do our churches nourish the brainforest? Thinking this way challenges us to move diversity in the church from the category of "nice to have" into the realm of commandment. I'll be the first to admit it can seem like a heavy lift to honor diversity as we fulfill Jesus' commandment to love one another. As a first step, we can take a moment to sit in awe and wonder. There is so much more to understanding the human brain than we ever imagined.

In God's brainforest, I imagine a giant sycamore tree of depression. Nearby is an ancient oak tree of anxiety. Just down by the forest creek is a baby pine tree of Autism. There is room for all of the trees to co-exist peacefully in God's brainforest. The ecosystem is diverse and healthier for being so diverse. Our communities are healthier when we support the inclusion and well-being of all brains, including those with mental health realities and disabilities. This is what the neurodiversity spiritual movement is all about—embracing God's radical inclusion of all brain differences within the neurodiversity movement.

Thinking about these words together—mental illness, mental health experiences, disability, neurodiversity, and neurodivergent—what relationship do they have to one another? Does the evolving understanding of the brain make void previous models like ill/well? Or can these words coexist and serve as nuances in the conversation? For the sake of including as many people as possible in the conversation, I encourage you to respect the language that feels right to the other person(s) as an expression of their own self-understanding. We can also be open to the fluidity of these identities, realizing everyone's identity changes over time.

Encouraging people to be free to self-identify is one way for Christians to show grace and understanding. Here are some examples:

1. Rey is in recovery from an eating disorder and describes herself as having a mental health diagnosis.

2. Kit has attention deficit hyperactivity disorder (ADHD) and identifies as both having mental health symptoms and as neurodivergent.

3. Taylor is Autistic and chooses to identify as neurospicy.

People may prefer the neurodiversity paradigm because it focuses on strengths rather than deficits. Stigma comes from defining people by their deficits. The neurodiversity paradigm still acknowledges that some brain differences can be experienced as deficits, but instead of focusing on the person having deficits, its focus is on demanding society play a role in helping to accommodate or support the neurodivergent person's needs. A neurodiversity paradigm acknowledges that our world is skewed toward people who are neurotypical, people who have brains that society's standards consider "normal" or typical. The benefit of the neurodiversity paradigm is that it emphasizes there is no normal brain because each brain is unique and special, like a fingerprint, the only one of its kind. We include mental health realities and disabilities within the neurodiversity movement as a way to help destigmatize brain differences.

Neurodiversity in the Church

When the church can think in terms of the big tent of terminology where each person is free to self-identify, then there is room for the full spectrum of self-understanding and expression of brain differences. Michael Paul Cartledge, co-author of the Princeton Theological Seminary's Brainforest curriculum, says to students in the program materials,

> The church really misses out when we don't reflect on and consider the unique gifts and strengths that each individual brings to the table, including neurodivergent young people, folks with ADHD, Autistic spectrum conditions, emotional and behavioral challenges. And what kind of unique gifts they have to offer in our congregations.

It is not the role of the church to diagnose people's mental illness or make assumptions about their identities; instead, the church can invite people into explorations and conversations about their identities as part of God's good creation. It is the church's role to extend an extravagant welcome to all and not to exclude people because of their differences. The evolution of our language to include neurodiversity is a sign that God is doing something new.

How might the church be blessed by considering the brain as an ecosystem, a brainforest, where diversity is the thing that makes it good, beautiful, and flourishing? Thinking of our brains and minds in this way can help the church see the value of diversity and break away from a focus on mental defects and disorders. We are less stigmatizing and shaming when we focus on the goodness of the diversity of the ways in which our brains work. This focus on the positive aspects of brain diversity allows us to appreciate and celebrate people who think and behave differently than what we consider typical, and it brings strength and gifts to our faith communities.

Christian teaching based on Genesis focuses on the goodness of God's creation. As part of God's creation, all human minds are created good, including the various ways we think and learn. As we explore these definitions of mental illness, mental health challenges, disability, and neurodiversity, I invite you to ask these questions: Could attention to language help my congregation become a place where all people can flourish? Does the language we use in my congregation contribute to neurotypical biases that limit our flourishing?

Biases are behaviors that exclude people who are different from belonging. Biases have specific names, too, like racism and sexism. Ableism is discrimination against disabled people. How might our understanding of the diversity of the brain, as part of Creation's good and natural diversity created by God, help us to show less stigma and discrimination toward people with brain disabilities and differences? Or could our support for neurodivergent folks be a key to our future?

Steve Silberman, in his article for WIRED magazine, said: "In forests and tide pools, the value of biological diversity is resilience: the ability to withstand shifting conditions and resist attacks from predators. In a world changing faster than ever, honoring and nurturing neurodiversity is civilization's best chance to thrive in an uncertain future."[18] Perhaps neurodiversity is the church's best chance to thrive as well.

Change can be difficult for all of us, perhaps especially for entrenched institutions like the church. Now is the time to be bold. Now is the time for community-building, truth-telling, and courageous action to bring about the changes needed for the church to flourish. Honoring and nurturing neurodiversity is part of God's plan for creation.

The Shadow-side of Neurodiversity

I wonder about the more difficult aspects of brain differences that may cause self-harm. What about when our brain difference causes us to feel hopeless and overwhelmed with life? What happens when our brain differences make it difficult to communicate with the people around us, causing us to feel isolated? What about when our brain differences compromise our physical and emotional safety? What about when our thoughts lead us to self-harm?

These are important questions to consider as we seek to understand the complexities of the brain and how best to support the flourishing of the brainforest. I find it useful to use the term neurodiversity in addition to, not instead of, language about mental illness, mental health challenges, mental health experiences, and disabilities because it incorporates the beneficial and the difficult—and sometimes devastating—realities of brain differences. Naming these complexities acknowledges how much we do not yet understand about the brain and the opportunities for continued learning, growing, listening, and sharing our stories and knowledge with each other.

My father's untreated bipolar disorder led to his early death. My brother's bipolar disorder led to his daily suicidal thoughts. My cousin's untreated mental health symptoms led to harmful behaviors to himself and others and eventually to his being imprisoned and executed. It does not feel true or honest to categorize the brain differences that contribute to harm of self or others under the umbrella of neurodiversity alone. I am open to this interpretation changing as I learn and grow, but for brain differences that lead to far more despair than joy, it's perplexing to think of these deeply painful realities as a part of a healthy ecosystem's diversity. Yet healthy rainforests include cycles of decay and death, reminding us that life includes processes of destruction. I wonder: Where is God in the midst of these realities? How can we seek comfort, compassion, and hope from our faith in times when our brains lead us to despair?

Does this mean that under the big tent of neurodiversity there is room for all aspects of the brain that seem to be directly related to human suffering? Are all mood and behavioral disorders, diagnoses, mental health symptoms, and mental health issues considered part of God's beautiful diversity, including ones that lead to death by suicide? Or do symptoms of mental health realities that cause self-harm come from various other biological or environmental sources, like how we think about the causes of cancer? Can a neurodivergent person hold multiple identities that make space for the aspects of brain differences that sometimes cause harm to the self? Not all neurodivergent people would identify as living with mental health symptoms. But people with mental health symptoms may identify as being neurodivergent. Making space for these complexities honors the diversity of our experiences. Each person's story of what it's like to live in their bodymind is important to respect, honor, listen to, and believe.

Faith communities can honor neurodiversity by striving to be loving, thoughtful, and respectful of people's autonomy and right to self-identify and to choose how they express themselves. If a person's mental health symptoms are causing concern about their own well-being or the community's well-being, it is important to have respectful and loving guidance for how best to provide the person with the support and resources they need. It is important to have accommodations so that true belonging may be attained. In settings like the church, can members of a congregation draw loving boundaries to reduce harm, and honor neurodiversity at the same time? What accommodations might help keep everyone feeling safe and free to be themselves? These are sensitive and important questions that need further discernment, conversation, and research with and by neurodivergent people

Thomas Armstrong is a psychologist who reframes many neuropsychological disorders as part of the natural diversity of the human brain rather than as definitive illnesses. In his book *Neurodiversity: Discovering the Extraordinary Gifts of Autism, ADHD, Dyslexia, and Other Brain Differences* he writes:

> We need to recognize that even though many people with neurodiversity suffer greatly and cause suffering to others, still, the existence of a diversity of minds in human culture is a basically a good thing because it provides civilization with a multiplicity of possibilities, a variety of styles of living, a number of unique perspectives on life, and a range of human potentialities that enrich our world rather than impoverish it, as would happen if we only had a narrow spectrum of human beings represented on the planet.[19]

Moving Neurodiversity from the Ivory Tower to the Steeple

As new ways of understanding the brain emerge out of academia, it's important for the church to continue to work to make meaning of these discoveries. Michael Paul Cartledge, Princeton Theological Seminary professor, explains to students in the course materials of his online course about neurodiversity about the origin of the neurodiversity movement. He says,

> Neurodiversity might sound abstract and academic, but it comes from the Autism community. Neurodiversity sees differences in brain function and behavioral traits as part of normal variation in the natural world. The neurodiversity perspective is often offered as a way to move beyond what has been called the pathology paradigm, focused on cognitive limitations. The neurodiversity paradigm vision is based on the natural variation in the ways humans think, learn, and live in the world.

It can seem radical to claim that what was once considered a flaw (such as stuttering or stimming, a form of self-stimulating behavior like arm- or hand-flapping, finger-flicking, rocking, jumping, spinning, twirling, or body movements) is God's way of expressing the full spectrum of diversity in creation.

I reached out to Cartledge for more conversation about his work creating the Brainforest curriculum and teaching a class at Princeton Seminary called "Neurodiversity, Faith Formation, and Young People." He believes the concept of neurodiversity is gaining popularity, especially among younger people, because neurodiversity "encompasses so many conditions and diagnoses that are often difficult to talk about in a general sense." He reminded me that the neurodiversity movement was born out of a socio-political movement to respond to injustice. This is an important feature of the neurodiversity movement because "it's a larger movement about commitment to justice and hope for change."

If you want to find people talking about neurodiversity, go to social media platforms. Young people are leading the way and talking about their own neurodivergence all over TikTok and Instagram. Because young people are engaging in what it means to be neurodivergent on social media, from the perspective of theological education, it makes sense to bring in the theological component into youth ministry.

Communities of faith need to wrestle with how we can grow in our compassion and love for people who have mental illness, mental health challenges, or disabilities or identify as neurodivergent—and their families. God calls the church to make spaces that can include and celebrate the stories of people who are neurodivergent as part of God's story.

Erin Raffety, an ordained minister in the Presbyterian Church (USA), with a PhD in cultural anthropology from Princeton University and co-creator of the Brainforest curriculum, says in her description of the program,

> This is an opportunity to really make sure the church is listening well to young people who are neurodivergent, listening to what they need to grow and learn, and excitingly, listening to what they have to teach us about God. I think that has the potential to change the church forever.

Now is the time for the church to respond faithfully to the rallying cry of the neurodiversity movement.

In the United Church of Christ there is a popular slogan inspired by vaudeville comedian Gracie Allen: "Never place a period where God has placed a comma. God is still speaking." Cartledge says, "The plus side of the growing neurodiversity movement is the raising awareness and talking about things that have been stigmatized." What might God be saying to the church through the various ways we understand, experience, and respond to mental illness, mental health challenges, mental health experiences, disabilities, and neurodiversity?

∞ Story Illustration

Here is an activity you can share with any age group to demonstrate what our blessed minds are like. The items needed are fresh cauliflowers and non-toxic paint. Paint different sections and different florets with how people feel their brain is wired. For example, some people may have large art sections of the brain, while others have small art sections. Other section ideas could be memory, computers, sports, dance, building, social, writing, math. When done with a group, participants can then look around at others and notice the variety of ways people have chosen to represent their brains. Painting cauliflower is a tangible, multi-sensory activity through which to engage in the exploration of neurodiversity. (For readers concerned about wasting food, the cauliflower may be added to compost if non-toxic paint was used.)

The blessed minds art project referred to above is based on an art project from the children's book *Brain Forest*. Here is its description of how brains are like forests:

Hey! Did you know that brains are like forests? … The Brain Forest is filled with unique brains, which makes it a beautiful thing. Can you imagine if there was only one kind of brain? Well, that would be booooring!! … Our brains work in different ways. It's called being neurodiverse. There are endless ways brains can be[,] right across the universe! Sometimes the things we're asked to do suit other brains more. When we ask everyone what they need, we know more than we did before. We can all make small changes that actually mean a lot. We can meet everyone's needs starting with listening and a little thought. Our brains need different things; it's not the same for everyone. With just little changes made, together we can have fun! …You are not alone. Find a therapist who is neurodiversity-affirmative in their approach and highly skilled in working with neurodivergent individuals. An affirmative therapist will partner with you (not try to fix you), celebrate your strengths, and help you as you work towards living a more authentic and meaningful life.[20]

? Reflection Question

What would your brain look like if you were to highlight and color the various parts of your brain that make you uniquely you?

 ### Neurodivergent Spirit of the Living God Prayer[21]

Cartledge uses the following prayer when he teaches his course about neurodiversity and faith formation at Princeton. He says it seems to speak to the lived experiences of his neurodivergent students, and he asked me to share it with you. The prayer's author is neurodivergent pastor Amanda Diekman, who self-identifies as an "Autistic contemplative."

Spirit of the living God,

fall afresh on me as I ask fresh questions of my life,

and seek out answers I've never sought before.

They say you made us by hand.

No machine or factory to mass produce humanity

which means you were there when my genes combined

when the alchemy of identity yielded one me,

in all eternity,

the first of my kind.

I've always felt different.

as though perhaps I came from a different planet

Dropped by accident

among a species so similar to me that no one can tell

from the outside

that I am not made of the same material.

Did you switch up the fabric for me somehow?

Did you choose a different shade of clay

without ever revealing your sleight of hand?

Now I ask questions like "Is there a name for people like me?"

And comb lists of criteria, assembled in intimidating order

in the Diagnostic and Statistical Manual of Mental Disorders, volume 5

a new holy text over which I pour my identity.

Will I settle into a patterned flow?

Do the drops of my story combine into rivulets, creeks, rivers,

flowing into enough evidence to achieve that holy grail,

diagnosis?

This book is filled with words that sting

"Abnormal"

"Fixated"

"Fails"

"Careless"

"Severe"

"Excessive"

These words worm into my secret places, sitting alongside the tender ones I hold close:

Beloved

Created

Desired

Redeemed

And yet I persist in my investigation, determined

desiring these labels to apply to me

because then I will know who I am

and who else in this great wide creation might be like me?

Is there a reason some things always feel so hard?

Is there a chance I'm not lazy, too little, too much, too broken, malformed, wrong?

My deepest longing is to know me as you know me,

so I beg you to guide my search with your eyes of grace

that I can see my inner terrain, filled with your fingerprints

marks of the artist's hand.

And if there is an Other Side for me

where I emerge, labeled, named,

may it be a homecoming to myself, a blessed resolution to a
lifetime of lostness

a new beginning

with a new tribe of fellow wanderers

who get what it is like

to be crafted from a different shade of cloth.

CHAPTER TWO

Ten Commandments of Neurodiversity

**Splashing the colors
From my own rainbow palette
Across the canvas**

 Neurodiversity Parable of Jesus' Rainbow Mind

It was the day after the storm, and Jesus was tired. He had spent all his energy calming the seas, and he had nothing left. Jesus was feeling anxious and needed some time alone. One way Jesus liked to relax was to sit beside the water and pray. Sometimes Jesus prayed using words, and sometimes Jesus prayed in colors, by painting with colors the different images that came to his mind.

This particular afternoon, Jesus splashed colors across the canvas scroll, making a rainbow. The rainbow reminded him of God's promise to love him no matter what, even if Jesus was too tired to heal other people or perform miracles.

Jesus just wanted some time alone to recharge his spiritual and mental batteries. Then Jesus remembered what his Father taught him about keeping the commandments of God. As Jesus gazed into the water, his eyes lost focus and the water began to blur in his mind's eye.

Jesus began daydreaming, wondering about the possibilities of other ways to honor God by honoring the diversity of creation. Jesus smiled as the image in the water came into focus. It was a reflection of a rainbow in the sky.

⌘━━╍ Key Words in Chapter Two

Ableism: A set of beliefs or practices that devalue and discriminate against people with physical, intellectual, or psychiatric disabilities and that often rests on the assumption that disabled people need to be "fixed" in one form or the other.[22]

Accommodation: Any product, adjustment, or service that makes a task or situation easier or more comfortable for someone to handle in their daily life.

Diversity: The range of human differences, including but not limited to race, ethnicity, gender, gender identity, sexual orientation, age, social class, physical ability or attributes, mental health realities, neurodevelopmental abilities, religious or ethical values system, national origin, and political beliefs.[23]

Inclusion: Recognizing and valuing the unique skills, talents, and experiences a person brings to the table.

***

Thou Shalt Honor Diversity

In some places in the United States, and in certain social circles, diversity is a highly debated topic. Here in central Indiana some public school boards are trying to ban books about diversity. In Florida the governor signed into law a bill banning diversity, equity, and inclusion initiatives in public colleges. I wonder: What are we afraid of when it comes to diversity? Why does anything outside of the range of the normative pose a threat to the status quo? What would the world be like if we honored diversity?

This chapter explores what might be possible if we followed the rabbi's lead and imagined what it would look like if we created a "ten commandments" for the neurodiversity spiritual movement. What might be the values, attitudes, rights, and freedoms we dream about for a just world for all when it comes to neurodiversity? These sample ten commandments are meant to stimulate your own creative thinking about spirituality and neurodiversity, in the playful spirit of the rabbi who invited his congregation with the question, "What if?" What if we could create a society where neurodiversity folks are truly honored and celebrated as made in the image of God? What spiritual and ethical teachings would guide us in our love and care for our neurodivergent kin? What if we had sacred guidance from the divine about neurodiversity? What would it say?

You may like some of these suggestions, or you may not. You may have ones that you would like to delete. You may have your own ideas about what would be best for you and your community. You may want to skip this section for now and come back later. The joy of being part of the neurodiversity spiritual movement is that we can be welcoming of diverse ideas, suggestions, and ways of understanding who we are as part of God's diverse creation. Each of the commandments ends with a creative prayer, inspired by my imagination of a Nurodivergent God.

Even though the Bible does not use the word "neurodivergent" to describe God, in my prayers, meditations, and reflections about the spirituality of neurodiversity, I am coming to experience the Spirit of God as neurodivergent. The Spirit of God is playful, whimsical, imaginative, complex, compassionate, deep, powerful, and good. May these spiritual reflections and prayers invite you to be open to imagining a new way of understanding and encountering the God of the spiritual neurodiversity movement.

First Commandment: You Shall Honor Diversity

Earlier, I mentioned that sociologist Judy Singer, who first published in an academic paper the term neurodiversity, once mused with her rabbi over whether there could be a better list of ten commandments than those Moses received from God on Mount Sinai. Inspired by this challenge, I dream about what it would look like to create Ten Commandments for Neurodiversity. Judy's blessed mind already gifted us with the first commandment: "You shall honor diversity." What does it mean to honor diversity? Some people see diversity as threatening because it is powerful or because honoring it could mean giving up power. Some people fear that honoring diversity could end up being divisive. Fear exists beneath every "ism" even to the point of transforming to hatred. But imagine if we allowed diversity to bring us together rather than to tear us apart. What would that be like?

To honor diversity is to be open to the blessing of the incredible variety of expressions of life. To honor diversity is to be unafraid of how God chooses to present themselves. To honor diversity is to be hopeful that God is still creating, God is still speaking, and God is still stimming. To honor diversity is to be humble about our own limited way of being, knowing that we can be so much more when we embrace one another's differences.

If Jesus gave a sermon today on the most important spiritual teaching—the ones about honoring God and loving your neighbor as yourself—what actions might Jesus suggest we do to fulfill those commandments? Or if God spoke through other prophets who have come along since the time of Moses, what might God's other nine commandments be, after "You shall honor diversity"?

 Reflection Question

What are some ways you can begin to honor neurodiversity within yourself or someone you know?

 Prayer

Still-stimming God, when we jump to judging, help us. Give us hearts of love so that we may honor neurodiversity as a gift from you. Amen.

Second Commandment: You Shall Rest as Resistance

The second commandment is inspired by artist and scholar Tricia Hersey, who encourages rest, saying "You shall rest as resistance." We will rest and stop over-functioning out of our own internalized ableism. In her Rest Deck, based on her book *Rest is Resistance: A Manifesto*,[24] Hersey says,

> The deprogramming from the brainwashing of grind culture begins in the quiet and powerful truth of your inherent self-worth. You are enough now. Can you slowly begin to believe this in the deepest parts of your heart and mind? Speak these words aloud, over and over again: "I am enough now. I can rest now."

We will rest and take off the masks we wear when we try to pass as "normal." We will embrace being weird. We will rest in the assurance that we are worthy of joy.

We will rest as a sign of our belovedness. We will rest because no amount of work will ever prove our value. After all, our value is not quantifiable. We will rest as resistance because we all deserve not only to survive but to flourish in all of our sacred neurodiversity.

 Reflection Question

What's the most exhausting part of living in a world that glorifies and worships being "typical"?

Prayer

God of rest, help us to honor the sabbath. When our minds are going a million miles an hour, bless us as we follow where the Spirit takes us in a flow state of mind. Thank you that rest and renewal is not always stillness. Thank you for dynamic ways we experience sabbath through movement, creativity, and play. Amen.

Third Commandment: You Shall Not Hide Your Light or Cover Up What Makes You Shine

The Bible's teaching to let our light shine brightly inspires the third commandment: "You shall not hide your light or cover up what makes you shine." Stigma grows in the shadows. Self-hate thrives in the shadows. Internalized ableism feeds off the shadows. Shame makes itself at home in the shadows. Coming out of the shadows is our right. We have a right to choose where we want to be, which means we do not have to stay in the shadows.

If we want to be in the light, we can come out of hiding. We do not have to cover up the very thing that makes us shine. We do not have to hide our neurodivergence. Neurodiversity can be shiny and bright when we *want* it to be, and when we *don't* want it to be, and that's not something shameful. Light is our superpower. It's an intangible energy that is a force we can harness to set ourselves free to be ourselves, a light shining in the shadows to help make the world a little bit brighter. Shine your light!

 Reflection Question

What causes the shadows of discrimination leading to the stigma and shame of having a brain that is different?

 Prayer

God of light, help us to be the light in a world that casts shadows of stigma and shame upon neurodiversity. Amen.

Fourth Commandment: You Shall Have Accommodations

The fourth commandment comes from the disability justice focus on accessibility for all: "You shall have accommodations to support your flourishing." If we truly want to create communities where everyone who wants to experience belonging is welcome, then accommodations will not be an afterthought. Noise-canceling headphones, fidget items, low lighting, large print, and elevators are just as necessary as the Bible and the cross. These are tools we use to create a beloved community, and without them we would feel as if something were missing.

What would it look like to embed accommodations into the template of church? Just as we cannot imagine coffee hour without coffee, what if we treated accommodations the same way? How could we have church without them? What if hospitality meant versatile seating options for church in-person, as well as accessible online ministry opportunities? Communities flourish when accommodations are understood as an important way we put our love into action and fulfill our mission.

 Reflection Question

What particular accommodation for spiritual spaces and faith communities would most benefit you or someone you love?

 Prayer

Fidget-spinning God, thank you for ways we can express ourselves without words. Thank you for the energy and power to move when we feel the Spirit. Amen.

Fifth Commandment: You Shall be Respected as a Whole Person

The fifth commandment highlights our freedom to define ourselves and not be defined by others: "You shall be respected as a whole person and not limited or defined by the ways other people assign you labels, diagnosis, or disease." There is nothing more stigmatizing than being labeled by another person or institution without your consent.

My brother, Scott, *is* not bipolar: he *has* a bipolar diagnosis. Instead of defining for others who they are, what if we invited people to identify and define themselves? And once they did so, what if we believed them and honored them? What is a positive and affirming use, if any, of labels that authentically reflect our chosen identity?

Why is it so hard for our faith communities to honor one another as whole people? To honor someone as a whole person does not mean we totally understand or even agree with them. It's OK not to understand why people express themselves or identify a certain way. It's none of our business. What *is* our business is sharing God's unconditional love and creating space for all expressions of personhood. One way we can work on doing no harm to others is letting go of our need to know everything. This need to know comes from our need to control others and our fear of what is different. We can let that go.

In quality customer service, business schools used to teach the "L.A.S.T." model for complaints: Listen, Apologize, Solve/Satisfy, Thank. But a "B" has been added to the new model, "B.L.A.S.T." The "B" stands for Believe. When someone tells you they identify as neurodivergent or what accommodations they need, believe them.

 Reflection Question

Recall a time when someone incorrectly labeled you. How did it make you feel?

 Prayer

God of infinite being, help us honor the wholeness and holiness of ourselves and one another. Amen.

Sixth Commandment: You Shall Be Included

The sixth commandment is based on values of inclusion: "You shall be included in all aspects of society and given equal opportunities for happiness and success." The goal of inclusion is belonging, being beloved as an important part of the community. One of the biggest risks in disability ministry is creating a disability ministry—that is, creating a special program for "the disabled people." In some congregations, this entails creating a separate worship service for Autistic children or creating a separate Sunday school classroom for disabled students.

This really misses the whole purpose of inclusion. To set people apart in separate groups is not inclusion. Even if the intention is good, creating disability ministries that are separate from the ministries of the church creates categories of otherness and exclusion.

What would it look like to make worship inclusive instead of having a separate worship service for people with disabilities? What if worship was designed from the outset with a neurodiverse congregation in mind? Inclusion in society and in the church means people with Autism, dementia, anxiety, ADHD, PTSD, and other brain differences are not an afterthought but part of the intentional design of what it means to be included in community.

 **Reflection Question**

Universal design is the idea that when we make the world accessible for people with disabilities, we make the world more accessible for everyone because we all benefit. Recall an instance in which you benefited from inclusion. What are some barriers to making faith communities more accessible and inclusive?

Prayer

Disabled God, help us make church more accessible for everyone. Amen.

Seventh Commandment: You Shall be Honored as Created in God's Image

The seventh commandment affirms the sacred origin of blessed minds: "You shall be honored as someone who is created in the image of the divine." Neurodiversity is a gift from God. We are neurodivergent because we are created in the image of the divine. We can honor one another and God by seeing the divine reflected in people who are neurodivergent.

We typically search for the cause of our differences and want to know what went *wrong*. We ask: "Why am I this way"? What if, instead, we claimed the divine blessing of being created in the image of our Neurodivergent God? To honor someone as having been created in the image of the divine means we value their diversity as a gift from God.

Our differences are not something to be changed, diminished, or ignored. We are not to love others or ourselves *even though* they/we are different or *despite* their/our differences. To honor neurodiversity is to see and acknowledge those differences and to learn from them. When we listen deeply to neurodivergent folks, I wonder what more we will learn? It is to feel the holy anticipation of how God's glory will reveal itself today in the blessed minds of our neurodivergent beloveds.

 Reflection Question

What does it mean to you that God is neurodivergent?

 **Prayer**

Neuroqueer God, thank you for creating all of us in your image, including people who stim, stutter, experience sensory sensitivity, are noisy and loud in church, and express themselves in ways other people do not always understand. Amen.

Eighth Commandment: You Shall Be Celebrated for Your Differences

The eighth commandment celebrates the giftedness of our neurodivergent minds: "You shall be celebrated for the different gifts you bring to the world." The diverse gifts of neurodiversity are not always celebrated. Sometimes people view neurodiversity as "too much." Too weird. Too uncomfortable. Too strange. Too loud. Too quiet. Too extra. Too big. Too small. Too shy. Too energetic. Too confusing. Too out there.

Instead, how about saying yes to celebrating all of it?

When we celebrate the gifts of neurodiversity, we create communities in which our gifts have a home. We can bring our gifts to the community and know that our community welcomes, values, and cherishes. At the same time, we don't always and freely have to share all of our gifts. We can just be. For example, instead of being the token creative person, we can be uncreative and uninspired. Being celebrated for our differences means that we are celebrated simply for being ourselves. Period. Even if we don't look or feel beautiful. We can be messy and feel down. And we are still valued as gifts to the community.

Reflection Question

What do you celebrate about neurodiversity?

 Prayer

God of rainbow sparkles, thank you for the joy of neurodiversity. Amen.

Ninth Commandment: You Shall Be Valued as an Asset and Not a Burden

The ninth commandment reminds us that our needs are not burdens: "You shall be valued as an asset and not a burden to society." One of the biggest challenges to creating communities that value neurodiversity is that it takes intentionality and it takes work. Because of stigma and ableism, because we have generally not designed our societies to embrace neurodiversity, this effort is a fight against the status quo. Some might say it is a burden they don't wish to carry. But if you are in a leadership role, making changes to the culture of your organization so that the organization's members understand and respond to neurodiversity as an asset and not a burden is simply the right thing to do.

To embrace neurodiversity requires that organizations adapt and change. Business as usual is not going to work for neurodivergent leaders. It is not a burden to supervise a person who is neurodivergent. It is not a burden to teach students who are neurodivergent. It is not a burden to create worship that honors neurodiversity. Inclusive communities that honor neurodiversity create enormous wealth in the health of their communities. The greatest asset of any organization is its people, including neurodivergent people. Imagine a world in which neurodiversity is your own and the world's greatest asset!

 Reflection Question

What aspects of brain differences can be experienced as a burden? Why?

Prayer

Autistic God, help us to embrace opportunities to honor the divine worth of each blessed mind. Amen.

Tenth Commandment: You Shall Be Free to Be You: To Explore, Grow, Create, and Change

The tenth commandment supports the full flourishing of neurodivergent minds: "You shall be free to be you: to explore, grow, create, and change." I believe another world is possible. I believe in a world in which we have absolute freedom—albeit with accountability and responsibility—to be the blessing God intended. God intended neurodiversity to be a blessing to the world. It's not God who limits us: we are the ones who limit ourselves and one another.

What would it look like if we were free to explore, grow, create, and change the world? Imagine the possibilities we could unlock in our neurodivergent minds. Such freedom exists in the absence of fear, shame, stigma, and discrimination. Such freedom exists in spaces that are safe from bullying, judgment, and hate. We can create communities where all people are free to reach their full potential. This is the future of which I dream for the children of the world.

 Reflection Question

What questions do you have as you learn more about neurodiversity?

 Prayer

Liberating God, thank you for beloved community where we can be free to unmask and flourish in all our neurodiversity. Amen.

CHAPTER THREE

Neurodiversity at the Bible's Beginning

**In the beginning
God didn't make a mistake
All brains very good**

Neurodiversity Parable of the Autistic Child and the Loaves and Fishes

Jesus was leaving the hillside and could still smell the fish and bread left over from feeding the five thousand. Jesus was feeling ashamed that maybe the sermon he had just preached had been a little too longwinded. He worried, "Were the women who got up during my sermon and walked away offended by something I said?"

Jesus tried to focus on the positive. He thought about the kind child who shared their fish and bread so others could eat. Jesus remembered noticing that as the child held the basket of food up to Jesus, the child's eyes looked up and off to the side. After Jesus thanked the child for sharing their food with the hungry crowds, the child smiled and began flapping, repeatedly tapping the sides of their body with both arms.

The child's mother, standing nearby, tilted her head to the side, smiled, and said to Jesus: "That's our beloved child. Some people say God made a mistake or they are that way because I sinned. My child's mind is blessed. God doesn't make mistakes."

Key Words in Chapter Three

Creator: God as the source of all created matter, the artist of all that exists past, present, and future.

Genesis: The first book of the Hebrew Bible/Christian Old Testament.

God: The one who is maker of heaven and earth and the focus of monotheistic religion.

Interconnectedness: The idea that nothing exists separate from anything else, that all of life is connected, and that what impacts one impacts all.

Spirit: The power of life that breathes into every living thing.

Trinity: The church doctrine that God is one but made of three expressions: God as parent, God as child, and God as Spirit.

***

Neurodiversity at the Bible's Beginning

What would happen if we read the Bible, a sacred book about God's love for us, through the lens of the spiritual neurodiversity movement? Through this lens, when I read the Bible open to the Spirit of our Neurodivergent God, I encounter the Bible as neurodivergent. The Bible is not a typical book! For a book that undergirds entire faith systems, it behaves atypically. Differences and divergence are everywhere in the Bible, starting at the very beginning of the book of Genesis. The beginning of the Bible is atypical for at least three reasons.

First, God self-identifies as being divergent in the divine expression as both Creator and Spirit. Second, there are two different creation stories in Genesis. Third, there is a full spectrum of diversity within the created order.

We can look at the whole Bible through a lens of neurodiversity, but I want to focus on the "beginning" stories here since they are so foundational to faith formation.

The Maker(s) of Heaven and Earth Are Neurodivergent

Christians who follow the doctrine of the Trinity think of God as three in one—God, Christ, and Holy Spirit or Creator, Redeemer, Sustainer. When they speak of God in Genesis, however, they usually refer only to God the Creator. God had company while creating order out of chaos. God expresses themselves in multiple forms. God is not your typical unified, singular divine being. Genesis 1:2 says that the power of God's Spirit, the mighty co-Creator, was also present; the "Spirit of God was hovering over the surface of the waters" (Genesis 1:2, New International Version). Another paraphrase of the Bible says, "God's Spirit brooded like a bird above the watery abyss" (Genesis 1:2, The Message).

The Hebrew word used for heaven is *rakia*, which means dome or vault.[25] The dome over the waters takes the shape of a womb, and God's

Spirit plays the role of midwife to God's birthing of creation. God is not alone. God reveals the wider spectrum of God's identities and self-expression. A diversity of gifts is used at the very beginning, and not all the gifts belong to God the Creator. God depends on the manifestation of the Spirit's gifts to give birth to creation. This story rides the waves of the energies born from chaos, a neurodivergent chaos, necessary for creation to reach its full potential.

As religion scholar Karla Suomala says, "What might happen if we [were to] use our God-breathed energies and talents in new, less combative ways? Such a model allows for less isolation and deeper connection for all life (human, plant, animal) with what in fact surrounds and envelops us."[26] If we can embrace the energies of chaos and trust them to guide us into fullness of life, then a neurodivergent creation story can lead to deeper connection. From the very beginning when God created the universe, it was neurodivergent and it was good.

Two Neurodivergent Creation Stories

In the Hebrew Bible, there is not one story of creation, but two different stories of creation. If you never noticed this, read the first two chapters of your Bible again—you'll see it. There's the story in which God speaks everything into being, taking one day for each element of creation. The narrative culminates in the creation of humans on day six. God famously rests on day seven. In the second story, the timeline of what God creates when is very different. The story culminates not with the creation of human beings but with the scenario of two naked human beings living unashamedly in the garden of Eden, before they are famously tempted to eat the fruit of a certain tree that God had warned them not to eat.

The existence of multiple creation stories illustrates the beauty of diverse stories and the power of more than one narrative. The Bible's diverse creation stories in the first and second chapters of Genesis invite us to embrace the overflowing vitality of the interconnectedness of creation. They paint the picture of the interrelatedness of God, humanity, food growing in the garden, and the whole creation that is marked by grace.

In Genesis 1:29–30, God's actions correlate to characteristics of neurodivergence with the overabundance of things, the excess of grace and provision, with the word "every" used five times in one verse. This emphasis on "every" and "everything" feels very neurodivergent to me. It speaks about a creation that is over the top—above and beyond what is called for, and at the same time just right and very good.

Our God is a neurodivergent Creator "and it was so." Genesis 1:29–30 says, "'See, I have given you every plant yielding seed that is upon the face of all the earth, and every tree with seed in its fruit; you shall have them for food. And to every beast of the earth, and to every bird of the air, and to everything that creeps on the earth, everything that has the breath of life, I have given every green plant for food.' And it was so."

God Filled the Earth with Neurodiversity and Said It Was Very Good

The third way the creation stories express neurodivergent qualities is in the fact that God makes two of every kind of animal and plant. The abundance of living creatures reflects the full spectrum of diversity in the created order of things. It is not enough to have one of every kind, but the genius of neurodiversity is the ability to recreate ourselves over and over again. We are not one and done. We exist in multitudes. We are never finished with expressing ourselves, and we refuse to stop evolving. Neurodiversity is part of every generation of creation, from the very beginning. Neurodiversity is part of creation's DNA.

What we know for sure is that neurodiversity plays out over generations of creation and existed from the very beginning of time, to today, and will be with us forever, into the future. We were created good, we are good, and we will forevermore be good.

The Bible tells the story of an atypical God who is not interested in keeping to the standards of what is considered normal or typical. God is expansive, creative, larger than life, and often too much. In the Bible, God breaks the rules of polite society, colors outside of the lines—and invites us to do the same.

Imagine all the other places where neurodiversity expresses itself in the Bible. If you look for it, you will see it everywhere. In the Old Testament, there are glimpses of neurodivergence if we read them with our heads tilted to the side for a new perspective. For example, in the third chapter of Genesis, Eve's encounter with the serpent gives neurospicy vibes, and Moses' communication troubles (stuttering) suggest he was neurodivergent. In the New Testament, given what the Gospel stories tell us about Joseph, Mary, and Jesus, a case can be made that the Bible tells the story of the Holy Neurofamily. In addition, the Psalms express the neurodiversity of the human mind, the full spectrum of emotions, thoughts, behaviors, and human reactions to the joys and tragedies of life. Where else does neurodiversity show up in the Bible? Imagine all that we might discover if we read the Bible through a hermeneutic lens, or interpretation, of neurodiversity! This is an area of biblical scholarship in need of attention.

Scholars like Raffety and Cartledge, and others, are uncovering the stories of neurodiversity embedded in the Bible, leading to new ways of thinking and talking about God that can help us live out our faith more fully. We'll explore God-talk, or theology, in the next chapter.

? Reflection Question

As you think about the stories in the Bible with which you are most familiar, where do you see sparks of neurodiversity? Which biblical characters express some neurodivergent characteristics, how, and why?

 ## Neurodivergent Creation Prayer

God of the stars and the moon, in the beginning when everything was literally a hot mess, you still called it good.

When we feel the chaotic rush to meet urgent deadlines, feeling overwhelmed and panicked, thank you for the whisper of your Spirit saying: "You don't need to do all the things in one day. It's OK. Take your time."

We praise you for creation's witness that good things evolve in slow, neuroflow time.

Help us to honor the sabbath to deeply rest our bodymind and make the sabbath sparkle with pleasure, playfulness, and joy.

When we feel like there is something wrong with the way our brain works, help us to remember that our brains are made in your divine image.

You say we are not broken.

You say we are good.

Bless our minds, Holy One.

Amen.

CHAPTER FOUR

A Theology of Neurodiversity

Whom do you worship?
The Neurodivergent God,
Who always loves me

⚮ Neurodiversity Parable of Jesus' Fidget Coin

Jesus fidgeted with the coin he found on the road on his way to Jerusalem. He liked having something to hold in between his thumb and his index finger. Having a fidget object helped Jesus focus his thoughts and relax. He pressed the coin in the palm of his hand. Jesus liked the way the pressure felt on his skin.

Jesus looked at the coin closely and wondered why people worshipped money instead of God. He knew that money would never love him back. Jesus also knew that God would always love him. He knew that having a neurodivergent mind was not a curse from God, but a blessing.

⚷ Key Words in Chapter Four

Fidgets: Objects that can be manipulated by the body. Their use is intended to aid in self-regulation and to help people improve their ability to focus and regulate feelings such as boredom, anxiety, and excitement. Fidgets serve a valuable purpose in the lives of people of all ages.

Theology: Conversations about God's relationship with humanity and all of creation.

***

A Theology of Neurodiversity

What is theology? Who creates theology? And whom does theology serve? Why do we bother with theology, and why is it worth our time? Why is theology an important part of the conversation about neurodiversity?

Theology is how we think, talk, dream, write, draw, sing, stim, flap, ruminate, fixate, fidget, create, dance, and imagine about God. Anybody can do this, from babies to the oldest person on earth. Theology is not just for Christians or trained scholars or ordained ministers. Theology by the people is the most powerful of all.

Theology serves society by giving us tools for serving the highest good. As humans, we aren't God; but as part of God's interconnected creation, we can do God's work. If God is love, then good theology comes from love and leads to love. A theology of neurodiversity is born from this movement of God's Spirit to make the world more loving. We do theology because the energetic force that compels us to love opens endless possibilities of using this energy for the good of humanity. It is worth our time to spread love when hate is on the loose. Theology is one way to harness this energy of the universe.

Theology is an important partner in the broader conversations about neurodiversity. From a theological perspective, neurodiversity is not a newfangled concept or a way to be politically correct. Instead, it has been part of existence since the beginning of time. The Bible shows that diversity is in the DNA of the universe. The very first two sentences of the Bible, in Genesis 1:1–2, when God created all that exists from the depth of the sea, diversity existed in the ecological environment of the sea. The DNA of creation is diverse. Why would the human brain be any less diverse than the rest of creation? God made humankind neurodiverse. And it is good.

A theology of neurodiversity helps us articulate why neurodiversity is not a problem to be solved but a good thing. Neurodiversity is not only to be tolerated, examined, and accepted as good business practice for human resources departments. Instead, neurodiversity is a matter of honoring the sacred worth of a unique human being created in God's image. God's creative genius is neurodivergent because God the Creator is not limited by or constrained to any single form.

A Disability Theology of Neurodiversity

Disability theology puts the bodymind experience of being disabled into dialogue with God-talk (or God-dance or God-dreaming). For too long, people have tended to understand disability in a too-limited way, for example, as referring only to those physical disabilities for which people use assistive devices such as a cane, walker, or wheelchair. If we instead consider neurodevelopmental disabilities, realities that affect brain growth and function, as equally important for consideration as physical disabilities, we include in disability theology the lived experiences of people who are neurodivergent.

The work of disabled theologian Nancy Eiesland in her book *The Disabled God*,[27] inspired new ways of engaging in disability theology that centered the voices of disabled people. Eiesland's writings paved the way for others to claim their expertise as disabled Christians and honor their personal stories as key theological ingredients in disability theology. Eiesland's claim that God is disabled invites the question: Is God neurodivergent? And if God is neurodivergent, what does that mean for us?

God Is Neurodivergent

A theology of neurodiversity that imagines God as neurodivergent is a worthwhile exercise because it creates space for dreaming. The Bible says we are created in God's image. Are neurodivergent people created in God's image, too? If neurodivergent people are created in God's image, then that means God contains neurodiversity within God's self.

If neurodiversity doesn't come from God, then from where does it come? A strong case can be made from interpreting the creation stories as we did in chapter three—that neurodiversity is a central characteristic of God's created order and that therefore God intends for neurodiversity to exist. Neurodiversity is of God.

Not only is neurodiversity a central characteristic of the created order, but perhaps neurodiversity is the capstone of all of creation. At the heart of God is neurodiversity. The mind of God is neurodivergent. The mind of Christ is neurodivergent. The mind of the universe is neurodivergent. And this is good.

A disability theology of neurodiversity proudly names our right to exist equitably with all others. We are not less than. We are not broken. We are not cursed. We are not to be pitied. We are not waiting to be saved. A disability theology of neurodiversity has the right to be included among other theological movements (such as liberation theology, womanist theology, and queer theology) in Christianity as we continue to evolve in the way we think, speak, talk, write, sing, and worship God. We need more opportunities to hear the thoughts, voices, ideas, and insights of neurodivergent theologians. I dream of a world where the labor and life of neurodivergent theologians creating theologies of neurodiversity are celebrated and included in all our God-talk.

 ## The Neurodiversity Prayer

In my church tradition, on Sunday mornings we pray together the prayer of Our Savior Jesus. This is the prayer that comes from the Bible story of Jesus teaching his disciples when they ask him how to pray. It is commonly known as "The Lord's Prayer." I have adapted the prayer here to imagine what the same formula would look like through the lens of neurodiversity. I invite you to use this prayer, making adaptions for your tradition. Or write your own version of The Neurodiversity Prayer.

> Our Neurodivergent God, who dwells in the multiverse, blessed be your name. Your beloved community come, your love overflow, on earth as it is in heaven. Give us this day our daily accommodations and deliver us from stigma as we release others from stigma, and lead us not into shame, but deliver us from ableism. For yours is the infinite flow of love, the power to overcome barriers to access, and the joy of belonging, forever and ever. Amen.

Story Illustration

I thank God for fidget toys and fidget bracelets and fidget keychains and fidget clothes. There must be a fidget theology because fidgets are how God calms me down enough, stills my mind enough so that I can hear the still speaking voice of God. Most days I wear multiple beaded bracelets on my wrist, and they are my spiritual fidgets. My bracelets are natural stones, representing diverse colors and textures and temperatures. These beaded bracelets help me to be present in the moment, especially when my mind wanders off and I begin to dissociate because of anxiety or fear.

A theology of fidgets honors the neurodivergent ways in which God reveals God's self through accommodations. Fidget theology honors the needs and experiences of our minds and bodies. Fidget theology prioritizes our mental health and emotional safety as the gateway to experiencing authentic and intimate connection to God. God shows up when we make theology more accessible because all bodyminds are welcome. I have multiple fidgets in my purse, in my car, and in my offices both at home and at church. I imagine the neurodivergent Jesus turning to his disciples and saying, "This is my fidget, given for you." I believe fidgets are holy and can be considered spiritual tools for prayer and communion with God. Not only traditional spiritual tools, such as prayer beads and rosaries, but ordinary fidgets can become holy instruments helping us focus on God's love for us.

Reflection Question

As you consider the many ways in which we can think theologically about neurodiversity, which theological concept is the most challenging to you? Why? How might God be calling you to make theology more accessible?

CHAPTER FIVE

Confronting Ableism and Stopping Stigma

Needing to be "fixed"?
Or learning to embrace you,
Your mind, your whole self

Neurodiversity Parable of the Ableist Disciples

The disciples called out to Jesus, who was praying alone in the garden. They shouted, "Come quickly! Come fix this family's child!" Jesus opened his eyes and looked up at the disciples.

Jesus asked, "What is it that the child needs?"

The disciples said, "The child's mind is broken. They do not talk. They do not look at anyone straight in the eyes. The only thing they do is spin around in circles!"

Jesus said to the disciples, "Yes, you are right to say the child needs help. But the child's mind is not broken. I called you to ministries of healing the sick. But this child is not sick. His mind is blessed and whole."

"But Jesus, this child is going to pass out from being so dizzy!" cried the disciples.

Jesus said, "This child is going to be thirsty and needs something to drink. Now go and get some water for the child."

Key Words in Chapter Five

Ableism: A set of beliefs or practices that devalue and discriminate against people with physical, intellectual, or psychiatric disabilities and that often rest on the assumption that disabled people need to be "fixed" in one form or the other.[28]

Discrimination: Being treated unfairly and unequally for a specific reason.

Shame: The feeling of being worthless, not good enough, or unlovable.

Stigma: The negative judgment of people due to particular traits or behaviors they have. Such judgment frequently prevents people from seeking mental health supports.

***

Confronting Ableism and Stopping Stigma

When it comes to conversations about mental health and neurological disabilities, one of the biggest barriers to inclusion and belonging is the two-headed dragon of ableism and stigma. Ableism is discrimination; it devalues people with disabilities. Ableism is when people with disabled bodyminds are seen as less than human. Ableism is when able-bodied people are considered to be superior to people with disabilities. Ableism creates a hierarchy of value and worth of human life based on perceived ability, with the most able-bodied at the top. Since ableism is society's unspoken expectation, disabled people are treated as inferior and experience stigma.

Stigma is a result of ableism. Because of discrimination toward disabled people, there is stigma: the shame of being categorized as less valuable, less worthy, and less than equal. Stigma is harmful because it excludes and punishes disabled people socially. The stigma related to mental health symptoms creates barriers to accessing support because the stigma causes people to isolate themselves for fear of social rejection. Stigma can be self-directed and at its most toxic can lead to self-hatred and even death by suicide.

Neurodiversity reframes the conversation of disability and mental health by providing a framework for dismantling ableism and stigma. Neurodiversity scholar Robert Chapman emphasizes the power of neurodiversity, not only as a grassroots justice movement but also as a philosophical concept. He himself has post-traumatic stress disorder and describes how the big tent view of neurodiversity can provide a helpful and liberating framing for many forms of brain differences. Chapman encourages an inclusive and expansive understanding of neurodiversity. He also believes the understanding of neurodiversity will continue to evolve over time. Chapman says the ultimate power of the framework of neurodiversity is

> How it helps us reimagine the world differently to how it currently is. For instance, it helps us both to reimagine pathologized and dehumanized minds in a more humane and compassionate way and to reimagine a world in a way that is less hostile to such minds. In turn, by adopting a neurodiversity perspective, we can alter actual relations; all the way to how we empathize with neurological others on a personal level.[29]

In short, we can destigmatize our brain differences through embracing neurodiversity.

If neurodiversity is part of God's creation and reflects the image of God, then a theology of neurodiversity provides the foundational view that disability and mental health differences are not weaknesses or flaws, but instead reflections of the gifts of a diverse creation. This fundamental view decapitates the two-headed dragon of ableism and stigma.

Imagine a world in which people are free to take off the mask and unreservedly show their neurodiverse identity. Imagine a world in which people of all ages can proudly be themselves, free to express who God created them to be, without fear of judgment, discrimination, stigma, and shame. Imagine the creativity that would be unleashed into the world if neurodiversity were allowed to flourish. Imagine a wild and free brainforest! When we dismantle ableism and stigma, we set free the full potential of the human body and mind.

Neurodiversity Paradigm as Suicide Prevention

Speaking of full potential: I wonder if having the support and safety, to be free from fear, stigma, and judgment, and to be able to self-identify as neurodivergent could save lives? If we agree with the claims that all people are created in the image of God and that all people are created good, this includes our minds as well. The diversity of human minds as part of God's good creation, instead of a curse, sin, punishment, or disorder, offers an alternative way for self-understanding and self-identity. For some people, the label of a mental illness or mental health diagnosis is a burden too heavy to carry. Thinking of oneself only as depressed, ADHD, bipolar, schizophrenic, anxious, or addicted can feel all-consuming.

For me, being labeled by my diagnosis—complex post-traumatic stress disorder—makes me feel as if I am being identified by my problems and past trauma. This label shines a light on all that went wrong, all that caused me pain, and all the hurt I still carry. Being able to self-identify as neurodivergent shines a light on the uniqueness of my mind as blessed by the Creator instead of being cursed. This is suicide prevention because we create new ways of telling our personal narratives, reclaiming who we are in the face of what attempts to destroy us and make us less than fully human. I have struggled with thoughts of self-harm since childhood and these urges come from self-hatred. What if I could learn to love myself more? This is the power of being able to self-identify as blessed, as part of a spiritual neurodiversity movement.

Ableism and stigma use these labels to limit people and create barriers to flourishing, whereas the named condition is only one part of who a person is. The brain is not only depressed: it is also many other things. Suicide happens when hope is limited by the shadows of despair. Labels limit us and can lead to despair.

Suicide is one of the leading causes of death in the U.S. In 2024 one person died by suicide every eleven minutes.[30] These numbers represent people: someone's child, partner, sister, father, and friend. It's time to break the silence about depression and anxiety being risk factors for suicide.[31] The neurodiversity movement can provide support, resources, friendship, and encouragement to people at risk of suicide because of mental health symptoms. Within the neurodiversity movement, there is hope through connection for people who feel ashamed, isolated, and alone.

One thing we can all do to increase hope is to share resources that support people who are facing mental health crises. In the United States there is a free, confidential 24/7 number that anyone can text or call to chat: 988. The 988 number will connect you to a trained counselor who can offer help and hope. Neurodiversity does not protect us from experiences of isolation, loneliness, and despair. It's important that we shine a light on this resource of 988. Please do what you can to help spread the word in your community about 988. I have a 988 bumper sticker on my car, and this simple act may help save a person's life. A friend saw just such a bumper sticker on a car while traveling. It said something like, "If you are looking for a sign to keep living, here it is: Call 988."

What if people diagnosed with mental health conditions were primarily celebrated as being members of an honorable, neurodiverse society? What if neurodiverse minds were appreciated for their complexity, their uniqueness, their value, and their contribution to the human family? How might the risk for suicide decrease among people with mental health diagnoses? How might suicide be prevented for people without a formal diagnosis, but who still experience symptoms? What if the framework of neurodiversity and belonging to a supportive neurodivergent community could help prevent suicide? What would that look like in your community?

Because ableism and stigma contribute to risk factors for suicide, embracing neurodiversity has the potential to serve as an additional form of suicide prevention. Celebrating neurodiversity decreases the stigma and shame of having brain differences. I believe that my niece's suicide could have been prevented if she had been able to identify her brain differences as part of God's good creation and if she had a supportive community that celebrated her neurodiversity and created a sense of belonging.

Unfortunately, the Christian church—ministers and lay leaders who were responsible for her faith formation—did not teach my niece that her mind was a gift from God. The church fails particularly its children, teens, and young adults at critical times of development by neglecting conversations about neurodiversity. These conversations about neurodiversity can benefit all ages, as a person is never too old to embrace a neurodivergent self-identity. In the absence of such conversations about the blessings of neurodiversity, children, teens, and young adults are left alone to question their differences and to wonder if who they are *is* actually good. Or if they are even *worthy* of life.

Can the Church Dismantle Ableism?

More conversations are unfolding within Christianity about ministries to dismantle ableism. In an article for *Christianity Today*, writer Sunita Theiss said:

> In 2018, a robust national study indicated that children with certain chronic health conditions are far less likely to attend church than their typically developing peers. Specifically, children navigating "invisible" disabilities such as Autism, anxiety, depression, ADHD, and other types of mental health issues and neurodivergence were the least likely to attend church. ...

> The church has the opportunity to radically transform our communities toward belonging—to make every aspect of the way we engage universally accessible and uniquely beautiful for every member of the body of Christ so that no person is limited from fully participating in the life of the church.

> Inclusion is not just a moral imperative: it is a lifelong spiritual practice. By intentionally creating spaces where individuals with disabilities are welcomed and celebrated, the church can

become a true reflection of the kingdom of God, where all are valued and all belong.[32]

My prayer is that the church would answer the call to faith by recognizing its role in preventing suicide. Embracing neurodiversity in the church can save lives because it dismantles the sins of ableism and stigma. As followers of Jesus, we have the power to expose the oppressive evils of ableism and stigma and the systemic shadows that perpetuate them. We cast out ableism and stigma by proclaiming the beauty, value, and blessedness of neurodivergent minds. We claim this in the name of the Neurodivergent God.

Ableism and stigma are death-dealing forces, propelled by the evils of discrimination. We know that in Jesus Christ good overcomes evil, and in the name of the Neurodivergent God we proclaim freedom from ableism and stigma. We celebrate that Jesus came to be among us so that we might have life, and have it abundantly, in all its neurodivergent glory.

Story Illustration

Stigma still happens in the church every day. Being stigmatized is a form of shaming, and it's particularly painful when it happens in the church, a community supposedly dedicated to loving one another. One experience of stigma and shame happened to me when I was a young mother and pastor.

Getting things ready at church right before worship began, I walked down the sanctuary aisle holding my child in my arms. My child wanted to stay close to me in a church filled with people he didn't know, so I carried him down the aisle, wearing my long black clergy robe. I often think of the Pietà and the powerful image of Mary holding the deceased body of her adult son, Jesus. It is holy to carry a child, no matter their age.

But the church woman in the pew was curious. Why, she wondered, was the pastor carrying her son, who was clearly old enough to walk by himself? She blurted out to me, "Pastor Sarah, is your son retarded?"

Reflection Question

What do you do when someone says something hurtful, stigmatizing, or shameful to you or to someone else in your presence? How would you have responded to the woman in church? How have you responded if/when you inadvertently said hurtful things to others in this manner?

CHAPTER SIX

The Neurodivergent Body of Christ

**Does it change me now?
Dyslexia, my power.
Mine forever more**

Neurodiversity Parable of Dyslexic Jesus

Standing in the middle of the village among a crowd of people, Jesus bent down and wrote something with his finger in the dirt. He moved his finger slowly, pausing in between words. But no one could understand what Jesus wrote. Jesus looked away from the dirt and looked up into the sky.

Jesus knew the power of God flowed through him. God's power felt to him like a warm, golden light. Even though Jesus' dyslexia confused some people, it didn't change the fact Jesus was filled with the neurodiverse power of God.

Key Words in Chapter Six

Accessibility: The Office for Civil Rights at the U.S. Department of Education defines accessibility as meaning "when a person with a disability is afforded the opportunity to acquire the same information, engage in the same interactions, and enjoy the same services as a person without a disability in an equally integrated and equally effective manner, with substantially equivalent ease of use."[33]

Body of Christ: The community of Jesus' followers who represent Jesus' hands, feet, heart, and mind in the world.

***

The Neurodivergent Body of Christ

What would you say if I told you the Body of Christ is neurodivergent? In addition to exploring how neurodiversity changes our understanding of the Bible and theology, we can also consider the ways it shapes our experience of being part of the Body of Christ. If neurodiversity is embedded in the created order and shapes our theological understanding of God, then it also shapes our experience of Jesus Christ in the body of believers. We create community in the Christian tradition when we come together as one in Christ. Honoring the neurodiversity of the Body of Christ means we are united by neurodiversity, not divided by it.

Neurodivergent people are already part of the Body of Christ. One in every four people lives with a physical disability, one in every five people lives with a diagnosable mental health condition, and one in every five people is neurodivergent. Depression is the most common form of disability in the world. We could say, given these statistics, that the Body of Christ is disabled, depressed, and neurodivergent. What does it mean for the church and for the ministries of the church that the Body of Christ is neurodivergent?

What does it mean to value neurodivergent members of the church as celebrated and equal members of the Body of Christ? What would it look like for the church to recognize its neurodivergent members as vital to the flourishing of the Body of Christ? What would it look like to celebrate the attributes of neurodiversity as gifts to, for, and of the Body of Christ? The Body of Christ is creative, resourceful, expansive, energetic, imaginative, playful, accommodating, thoughtful, and diverse. The true power and beauty of the Body of Christ is unlimited through the lens of neurodiversity. There are vast and rich gifts waiting to be named, included, and celebrated in the Body of Christ.

The symbolism of the church as the Body of Christ alive in the world helps us understand our interconnectedness and dependence upon one another. To embrace neurodiversity in the Body of Christ means we create space and encourage new opportunities for diverse expressions of God's Spirit. Through the Body of Christ, the neurodivergent Spirit of God is still at work in the world, bringing forth something new.

Resurrecting Neurodiversity in the Body of Christ

The neurodivergent Body of Christ is not struggling, decaying, or dead. The resurrected Christ is neurodivergent. The resurrected Spirit of God energizes the body of Christ, inspiring the expansiveness of neurodivergent embodiment. Anything is possible with a neurodivergent embodiment of God. Imagine how a youth group might be invited to embody the neurodivergent Body of Christ. What might we learn from a youth group with neurodivergent youth about the Body of Christ?

What if the ideal Body of Christ was not our general stereotype? What if the ideal Body of Christ, the resurrected Body of Christ, was neurodivergent? How might our understanding of church be changed if we embraced the Body of Christ as neurodivergent?

The Body of Christ represents our understanding of Christ's community alive in the world. What would it look like if we assumed that the Body of Christ is neurodiverse? It's one thing to interpret a sacred text and to talk about God's neurodivergence; it's another thing to apply these interpretations to describe the community of people following the way of Jesus today.

There is nobody that does not belong. In Christ there is neither typical nor atypical, neither neurodivergent nor neurotypical. We are all one in Christ Jesus. What's wrong with being different? Why are differences often viewed as bad or less valuable?

What if neurodiversity is what God has always called good and the church has simply misunderstood that until now? God never meant all of us to be the same. It was never a punishment from God to be different. It was always a blessing.

God, forgive us for the harm we have done in the name of conformity. God, help us to live more fully into the holy calling as the neurodivergent Body of Christ.

Any Body, Every Body, Christ's Body

The United Church of Christ, a Protestant denomination in which I have worked for many years, embraces disability and mental health as important parts of the neurodiverse Body of Christ. United Church of Christ minister Rev. Dr. Harold Wilke is a pioneer in the disability ministry movement and faced his own experiences of ableism and discrimination inside and outside of the church. He was part of the national leadership as a faith leader during the passage of the American Disabilities Act in 1990. Sharing his thoughts about disability and the Body of Christ, in a 1977 article for *Christian Century*, Dr. Wilke wrote about the need for the church to be accessible:

The Church's unity includes both the "disabled" and "the able." A church which seeks to be truly united within itself and to move toward unity with others must be open to all; yet able-bodied church members, both by their attitudes and emphasis on activism, marginalize and often exclude those with mental or physical disabilities. The disabled are treated as the weak to be served, rather than as fully committed, integral members of the Body of Christ and the human family; the specific contribution which they have to give is ignored. ... The Church cannot exemplify "the full humanity revealed in Christ," bear witness to the interdependence of humankind, or achieve unity in diversity if it continues to acquiesce [to] the social isolation of disabled persons and to deny them full participation in its life. The unity of the family of God is handicapped [when] these brothers and sisters are treated as objects of condescending charity. It is broken where they are left out.[34]

Following this foundational work, in 2005 the Twenty-Fifth General Synod of the United Church of Christ adopted a resolution calling congregations and other ministry settings of the UCC to develop accessibility and inclusion plans. Over the years many efforts to build ramps and undertake other physical improvements took place. However, the UCC Disabilities Ministries Board of Directors noted that eleven years later several congregations that had started accessibility work had halted their movement forward. Citing research that showed social attitudes are often a bigger barrier to inclusion than cost, the Disabilities Ministries Board in 2016 published a resource for congregations wishing to be more accessible, engaging, and inclusive for disabled people.

"Any Body, Every Body, Christ's Body" is a free, online guide that helps congregations learn about the theological and practical reasons for congregations to become accessible to all. In the introduction the authors write,

We live in an increasingly complex world, and the complexities of this world include the reality that one in five persons lives with a disability and one in four persons experiences a mental health concern over a lifetime. In John 13:34 (NRSV), Jesus declares: "I give you a new commandment, that you love one another. Just as I have loved you, you also should love one another." Within the UCC we can find new ways of loving one another when we expand our hearts, minds, and actions.

∞ Story Illustration

One of the most awkward selfies I ever took is a photo of me standing at a truck stop along the highway in the late afternoon sun. In the photo, I smile, but I am post-migraine and road weary. I'm masking my pain. I am wearing a teal and black silk blouse and holding an award plaque I received at the national convention from which I was driving home. The award was in honor of my mental health ministry with the United Church of Christ Mental Health Network. That photo stands out in my mind because just prior to accepting the award at the convention center luncheon, I was in the bathroom down the hallway throwing up. I remember texting the organizers to let them know about my sickness. They moved the award ceremony from after the luncheon to the beginning of it so that I could receive the award and then go back to my hotel room to sleep off the migraine.

I remember feeling ashamed. I thought, "What's wrong with me? What kind of loser am I that I can't even get it together to accept this award? I'm a fake. I don't deserve it." The overstimulation of the thousands of people at the convention, the bright overhead fluorescent lights, the constant social interactions, the long days and short nights all teamed up to shut down my brain. Thinking back to what happened, I feel more compassion for myself than shame. I was too hard on myself. I pushed myself too hard. I was wearing the mask hard.

What would it look like if in the church we could be softer, softer with ourselves and with one another? What would it look like if we gave ourselves permission to claim grace for ourselves, the same amount of grace that we are sometimes much more willingly to show others? This question led me to begin dreaming about new and different ways of being church that honored our bodymind and took seriously what weeklong national conventions do to our bodyminds. Working with the UCC Disabilities Ministries Board and the UCC Mental Health Network, we began to create community care and self-care spaces at our national gathering. They have low lighting, soft places to sit, blankets, couches, chaise lounges, fidgets, prayer shawls, yoga mats, and quiet.

With other people's help, together we designed the space I needed so I, and others like me, could be part of the church and not hide in the hotel room. Of course, it turned out many others needed this space, too. We continue to create this kind of space, and it is meaningful to the many people who are seeking sanctuary that honors their blessed minds, their neurodiversity, as an important part of what it means to be the Body of Christ.

? Reflection Question

We don't treat our brains very well. We treat our brains like machines, high-functioning computers or snack vending machines. Even machines need to be rebooted, powered down, and recharged. Our brains are so much more. We demand so much of our brains. What would it look like instead to honor our own minds as the neurodivergent Body of Christ, treating them with care, compassion, and respect?

CHAPTER SEVEN

Neurodiversity and Intersectionality

Hidden persona
Behind a mask: a blank smile
None know the real her

⬭ Neurodiversity Parable of Unmasking

The Samaritan woman learned to hide her multiple intersectional identities behind a mask. This is how she kept herself unseen and safe. She wasn't sure whether Jesus would want to know the real her.

But when she met Jesus at the well, she was able to come out of hiding, and her life changed forever. Jesus saw her for who she truly was, without a mask. And Jesus blessed her.

She blessed Jesus, too, by drawing cool water for him to drink. Two blessed minds found a sense of belonging and interconnection at the well.

⚷ Key Words in Chapter Seven

Decolonizing: The process of challenging and dismantling systems that perpetuate supremacy, power, and privilege.

Equity: Providing resources appropriate to the environment to obtain equal outcomes. Imbalances within our social systems result in a need to provide equitable processes.

Intersectionality: The existence of interlocking forms of oppression and their impact on people's lives.

Neuroqueer: A person who sees their neurodivergent and queer identity interacting and working together in a way they wish to claim/self-identify with.

***

Neurodiversity and Intersectionality

A prominent symbol for neurodiversity is an infinity loop with a rainbow-colored palette, as featured on the cover of this book. When we think about how neurodiversity intersects with other forms of diversity, this symbol represents limitless possibilities. There are infinite ways in which humans express and experience diversity. There is a saying in the disability community that when you meet one Autistic person, you have met one Autistic person. No two people with Autism are the same. This concept of diversity applies to other categories of difference too.

The neurodiversity movement belongs in intersectional spaces. Neurodiversity scholar Lauren Rose Strand says,

> Intersectionality is critical for Disability Studies scholars and activists because both intersectionality theory and Disability Studies seek to make the less-visible or under-recognized, visible and because both seek to call into question privileges and disadvantages that have historically resulted in some individual and collective bodyminds being marginalized.[35]

Strand invites us to continue to engage in explorations of neurodiversity as intersectional, especially because of the potential power in coalition-building. Imagine if all the LGBTQ+, BIPOC (Black, Indigenous, People of Color), and disabled neurodivergent folks united to work for justice for all!

The power of thinking about intersectionality is the emphasis on how our differences are positives, not deficits. Diversity is important to our identities. The challenge with representation when it comes to diversity is that no one person can represent their gender, culture, race, disability, or identity. And it is not fair to ask this of them, for this disrespects the person and the communities God has called us to serve and to empower. Too often it seems as if organizations, including seminaries and churches, are merely seeking to check off boxes when it comes to diversity. Our identities are more complex than this narrow view of human difference. The same is true with neurodiversity, and that is why the symbol of the rainbow infinity sign is so powerful.

Blessed Intersectionality

In the late 1980s, a decade before academically published thoughts about neurodiversity emerged, Black feminist and critical race scholar Kimberlé Crenshaw introduced the term "intersectionality" to illustrate how people experience discrimination differently and in complex and overlapping or intersecting ways, depending on their identities and the degree to which each identity affords social privilege within power structures. At the time, Crenshaw was studying the lives of women of color, particularly immigrant women, and their experiences of surviving domestic violence. Crenshaw discovered that immigrant women confronted both "structural intersectionality" as well as "political intersectionality," creating higher risks for them to experience domestic violence.

Crenshaw observed that the 1990 Immigration and Nationality Act (USA) forced immigrant women seeking citizenship or permanent residency to stay married to and live with their U.S.-citizen or permanent-resident spouses, regardless of experiences of domestic violence. In this example, both the state and the spouses created oppressive structures for women that intersected with their gender, class, and national origin.

Crenshaw also described the phenomenon of mainstream feminism being dominated by and catering to the experiences of White women. Its effect was to push the needs of women of color to the margins of political discourse. Crenshaw's research identified that the intersection of racism and sexism prolonged the domestic and sexual abuse experienced by survivors who were women of color.

A very basic example of intersectionality would be to consider the experiences of a Black woman, a Black man, and a White woman. The Black man may be oppressed by racism because he is Black, but he enjoys the privilege of being male. The White woman may be oppressed by patriarchy because she is a woman, but she enjoys the privileges of being White. However, the Black woman experiences the intersection of both racism and patriarchy, so she is exposed to systemic discrimination and oppression at a higher level than both the Black man and the White woman.

Add to this example Autism. Here we have the life experiences of a Black man, a White woman, and a Black Autistic woman. In addition to the intersection of racism and patriarchy, the Black woman also experiences the negative impact of ableism.

Honoring the various forms of intersectionality is one way to honor the multiple identities a person experiences in the world, and how these identities shape their access to equal rights and freedom from discrimination.

I say intersectionality is blessed because when we honor the multiple identities a person experiences, we have an opportunity to work for justice and equality. Intersectionality is blessed when we honestly engage in the work to dismantle individual and communal systems of oppression. Our Black Autistic sister is a blessing. She is not *a* problem or *the* problem. She is a blessing. It's our individual and communal biases and discrimination that are the problems. Acknowledging racism, sexism, ableism, heterosexism, transphobia, ableism, and other forms of systemic oppression means that we must address these biases both individually and collectively as a church.

Intersectionality in the Bible

The fourth chapter of the Gospel of John tells the story of Jesus' ministry to people with multiple intersectional identities. Early in Jesus' ministry, when he was returning to Galilee, Jesus stopped in the town of Sychar in Samaria to rest by a well while the disciples went into town to get food. As Jesus was resting, the Samaritan woman came to fetch water, and Jesus asked her for a drink. She was surprised at Jesus' request, for Jews did not associate with Samaritans. Jesus responded that if she knew who she was talking to, she would have asked Jesus for a drink.

Commenting on this passage, Amy Crawford, a diaconal minister in the United Church of Canada, says,

> Jesus sees the Samaritan woman and considers her entire identity. He doesn't just see her as a woman to whom he shouldn't be speaking alone (note the disciples' reaction in verse 27). Jesus doesn't just see her as a Samaritan, whom he has been taught to avoid (verse 9). He doesn't just see her as someone with a complicated relationship history (verses 16–18). Jesus sees all of who she is—a woman, a Samaritan, one who has been marginalized because of her many marriages and relationships—and reveals his own identity to her.[36]

In this Gospel story of intersectionality, we are given specific details about the Samaritan woman. Perhaps the author intended us to be able to honor all of her identities and to respect her life experiences of societal oppression, prejudice, and shaming. In this story we see her multiple identities emerge: she is a woman, she is a Samaritan, and she is in relationships with multiple men. None of these identities makes her less worthy of Jesus' friendship, compassion, and love. Crawford says, "Jesus doesn't ignore or erase her identity. Instead Jesus meets her at those intersections. She is deeply known and accepted, and [is] empowered to become a messenger of hope to her own people."[37]

When it comes to blessed intersectionality, we too can be confident that our whole identities matter to the God who formed, who created us in God's own image, and chose us. Crawford says, "An intersectional reading of this text indicates that even as we embrace a shared identity in Christ, it is important to note that the layers and intersections of identity increase the church's prophetic imagination, strengthen its witness, and enhance our advocacy."[38]

Neurodiversity and Disability Justice

It is time to include neurodiversity in conversations about intersectionality. And to do so in equity with all facets of intersectionality. Often overlooked, especially in discussions about diversity, equity, and inclusion, neurodiversity represents important identities of people who experience discrimination and oppression. A member of the United Church of Christ Disabilities Ministries Board named Helen Walsh was recently asked to serve as a volunteer leader with Voluntary Organizations Active in Disaster. Because of her advocacy, Voluntary Organizations Active in Disaster decided to add accessibility to their work of diversity, equity, and inclusion. When we honor the full expression of people's multiple identities, we more faithfully accommodate their needs and make important services, like disaster response, more accessible.

Disability and mental health justice intersect with neurodiversity. Working to end ableism, discrimination, and inequality requires a better understanding of how neurodivergent people are subject to bias and prejudice. This is an area that lacks research, and therefore we do not yet fully understand how neurodiversity shapes a person's experience of injustice. The power of conversations about neurodiversity is that they honor the various ways in which people experience the world, considering how they process, perceive, communicate, and navigate the world differently.

Neurodiversity and Racial Justice

I first met Dr. Kimberly Douglass when she was teaching an online course on "Decolonizing Neurodiversity" for Eden Theological

Seminary. Douglass is the full-time owner of Kimberly Douglass, PhD, LLC, through which she and her team are designing a world in which neurodivergent people feel they belong. She is a Black mother of a neurodivergent son and, thanks to her experience with him, has gotten in touch with her own neurodivergence. She says, "My work is THE foundation for decolonizing the lived experiences of Autism, ADHD, learning disabilities, Bipolar Disorder and other neurodivergences. ... Decolonizing neurodivergence is a community effort." She grew up in a Black Baptist Church and was told she "shouldn't speak up for herself" and thus saw Christianity as a tool of enslavement.

As a student in Douglass' class, I appreciated her depth of analysis at the intersections of racial justice and disabilities and mental health justice. My first introduction to the brave new world of neurodiversity was in the church, specifically in the spheres of theological education. The graduate course description said,

> A Neurodiverse God would have us recognize how White supremacy impacts the lived experiences of Neurodivergent People (ADHD, Autism, Sensory Processing Disorder, giftedness, learning disabilities and others). Neurodivergent People of Color will be of special interest as we engage and deconstruct religious and other social systems that reinforce the relationship between White supremacy and the negative outcomes for Neurodivergent People.

Douglass says:

> Ignoring neurodiversity will allow you to stay right where you are. ... [Twenty-first century leadership is] community-centered, creative, curious, decolonizing, and neurodivergent. ... Neurodiversity is truth-telling about how people really are, what people really need. Leadership for 2023 and beyond must be about perceiving, responding to and attempting to meet the needs of the broadest range of people.

Her advice?

1. Neurodivergent perspectives are critical to the leadership we need to address the complex challenges we face in society (and the church). And to meet complex needs. Leadership by neurodivergent people provides meaningful solutions for a broad range of people.

2. To step into leadership roles (meeting human needs) Neurodivergent People have to be willing to deconstruct, decolonize, and heal—to reduce harm to ourselves and to others. We cannot use others as distractions from our healing. A decision maker that is not committed to their own healing process WILL create harm to themselves and others. They will marginalize and further marginalize people.

3. Leadership is a community activity.[39]

About the intersection of neurodiversity and power she has this to say:

Just considering the sensory needs within the Neurodiverse community shifts power to community members. It shifts who can get support. It changes the calculus of whose needs are considered legitimate and urgent. In the U.S. society personal needs are seen as less legitimate than the needs of corporate and state systems. Thus, human lives are surveilled for productivity, not to understand human needs.[40]

As faith communities striving to operate under the return on investment of loving our neighbor as ourselves, we can flip the script of a society striving for productivity. What if people of faith prioritized personal needs above corporate needs?

 Prayer in Praise of Intersectionality

Dr. Douglass wrote the following prayer as part of the United Church of Christ and the United Church of Canada worship resource for Mental Health Sunday:[41]

God of Biodiversity, God of a biodiverse world, God of a neurodiverse people:

We pray for communities that value neurodiversity.

We pray for communities that embrace diverse thoughts and ideas.

We pray for communities that make physical space for neurodiverse individuals.

We pray for communities that recognize neurodiversity as a community asset.

We pray for organizations that can hear us, see us, and respond to our neurodiverse needs.

We pray for organizations that serve, that care, that love.

We pray for organizations that respond to us simply because we say we have a need.

We pray for organizations that adapt to human needs.

We pray for people who look past our behavior to understand the needs that drive our behavior.

We pray for people who understand that behavior is a communication tool.

We pray for people who are willing to sacrifice their comfort to protect neurodiversity.

We pray for people who have the courage to challenge the systems that reduce neurodiverse needs to right and wrong.

We pray for stories that help a neurodiverse society see itself.

We pray for stories in which neurodiversity is a cause for celebration.

We pray for stories in which people are complex.

We pray for stories in which neurodiversity makes us hopeful about the future.

We pray for stories that make us weep at the loss of neurodiversity.

In your biodiversity, we see the truth of your grace.

Thank you.

In your neurodiversity, we see the promise of your love.

Thank you.

Amen.

Neurodiversity and LGBTQ+ Justice

Members of my own extended family have experienced the pain of discrimination from the church when it comes to gender identity and sexuality. Faith communities that shame people for expressing themselves create emotional harm and long-lasting trauma. Julie Nichols is an educational therapist/vocational rehabilitation specialist, a contemporary

Catholic writer, and a part-time advocate for neurodivergent and LGBTQ+ youth. She writes:

> The reality is this: Treating LGBTQ and neurodivergent families with decency, respect, and equality has proven to yield good fruit—joy, peace, mental health, stability, and a longer lifespan—while religious ideas that encourage the church to exclude or shame neurodivergent and LGBTQ young people produce depression, anxiety, self-hatred, shame, self-harm, substance abuse, separation from God and the church, isolation, anger, serious mental illness, and even suicide. In short, when the church does not accept families like mine, it is, though perhaps unwittingly, complicit with actions that cause us harm.[42]

Indeed, the LGBTQ+ community is an important part of the neurodiversity movement. Research from the University of Cambridge found that Autistic people are eight times more likely to identify as LGBTQ+. Studies by The Brain Charity, a British disability and mental health service and advocacy nonprofit based in Liverpool, found that in the wider neurodiversity community, significantly more people self-identify as LGBTQ+. One person who identifies as Autistic and LGBTQ+ explained the intersection this way:

> With being neurodivergent, a lot of people already challenge the status quo when it comes to social traditions and social rules, so what's to say that the way they love is any different? ... It's important that we bring attention and care to people who are neurodivergent so they understand that they deserve to be loved, regardless of their traits and characteristics.[43]

The prejudice toward neurodivergent folks means that sometimes we assume they are not capable of understanding or expressing their own sexuality and/or gender identity. According to The Brain Charity, one-third of those surveyed said their gender identity was repeatedly questioned because they were Autistic. This led researchers to postulate that there is an underdiagnosis of neurological conditions among the LGBTQ+ community.

According to The Brain Charity, one of the leading theories as to why there is an intersectionality between neurodivergent and LGBTQ+ communities is that neurodivergent people tend to be less influenced by social norms of a binary society where being heterosexual and cisgender are the default. Neurodivergent people might feel freer to express their gender and/or sexuality and less concerned about meeting society's expectations.

For both the LGBTQ+ and the neurodivergent communities, there is still significant stigma from society and in the church. Some folks still attempt to "cure" people of being queer or Autistic, and this causes them emotional and spiritual trauma. Societal stigma and discrimination increase the experiences of anxiety and depression in both the queer and the neurodivergent communities. John Anderson of The Brain Charity reminds us that

> There is so much joy to be found in acceptance and pride, whether accepting your neurodivergence as a strength and an inherent part of you, or coming to terms with your true gender identity. The world is slowly catching up. We will continue working for a society that fully embraces what both neurodiversity and the LGBTQIA+ spectrum have to offer.[44]

I quite intentionally invite faith communities to bless people at the intersection of neurodivergent and queer identities. Given the historic harm and trauma that the church has inflicted upon LGBTQ+ communities, those seeking to build trust should take the opportunity for self-examination. The reality is that when we in the church shame, isolate, judge, and cast out the queer community, we are doing so to many people who are neurodivergent as well. To embrace the neurodivergent community is to embrace the queer community. When God created humankind in God's image, God created us neurodivergent and queer. And God said it was good.

Dr. Nick Walker, author of the book *Neuroqueer Heresies* and professor of psychology, coined the term "neuroqueer" in 2008 and talks about the "neurodiversity paradigm." He says:

1. Neurodiversity—the diversity among minds—is a natural, healthy, and valuable form of human diversity.

2. There is no "normal" or "right" style of human mind, any more than there is one "normal" or "right ethnicity, gender, or culture."

3. The social dynamics that manifest in regard to neurodiversity are similar to the social dynamics that manifest in regard to other forms of human diversity (e.g., diversity of race, culture, gender, or sexual orientation). These dynamics include the dynamics

of social power relations—the dynamic of social inequality, privilege, and oppression—as well as the dynamics by which diversity, when embraced, acts as a source of creative potential within a group or society.[45]

Walker confirms that, for the queer community,

> The Neurodiversity Movement is a social justice movement that seeks civil rights, equality, respect, and full societal inclusion for the neurodivergent. The Neurodiversity Movement is not a single group or organization … and has no leader. Like most civil rights movements, the Neurodiversity Movement is made up of a great many individuals, some of them organized into groups of one sort or another. These individuals and groups are quite diverse in their viewpoints, goals, concerns, political positions, affiliations, methods of activism, and interpretation of the neurodiversity paradigm. The Neurodiversity Movement began with the Autism Rights Movement.[46]

Walker also helps unpack the use of the word "mind" when speaking about neurodiversity. This is the same understanding I have in my use of the phrase in the book's title, *Blessed Minds*. Walker says,

> In speaking of neurodiversity as the diversity among minds, I use the word mind in the broadest possible sense, to encompass the totality of every aspect of perception, cognition, emotion, memory, psyche, and consciousness. Mind is an embodied phenomenon. The activity and development of the mind has a physical component in the form of electrochemical activity in the brain; the mind is encoded in the brain as ever-changing web of neural connectivity.[47]

Walker defines neuroqueer as:

1. Being both neurodivergent and queer, with some degree of conscious awareness and/or active exploration around how these two aspects of one's being entwine and interact (or are, perhaps, mutually constructive and inseparable)

2. Embodying and expressing one's neurodivergence in ways that also queer one's performance of gender, sexuality, ethnicity, and/ or other aspects of one's identity

3. Engaging in practices intended to undo and subvert one's own cultural conditioning

4. Engaging in the queering of one's own neurocognitive process

5. Approaching, embodying, and/or experiencing one's neuro-divergence as a form of queerness

6. Producing literature, art, scholarship, and other cultural artifacts that foreground neurodiversity

7. Producing critical responses to the above

8. Working to transform social and cultural environments in order to create spaces and communities—and ultimately a society—in which engagement in any or all of the above practices is permitted, accepted, supported, and encouraged.[48]

Considering this expansive and helpful description of neuroqueer, I wonder how our faith communities can be communities in which people can express and experience neuroqueer ways of being? What would it look like for a church that is already open and affirming for LGBTQ+ communities to work quite deliberately to create neuroqueer ministries? How might God's Spirit be inviting the church to create opportunities for open conversations about neurodivergence and LGBTQ+ communities to help foster greater understanding to prevent harm?

  Breaking the Silence with Neuroqueer Prayer

Alicia T. Crosby posted a short video on her social media page to share a prayer she wrote that she believed would bless a larger audience. She was right. And she gave me permission to share with you the words to her prayer. Alicia identifies as Black, queer, and neurodivergent and is a justice educator, activist, and minister who helps others explore and unpack topics related to identity, justice, journey, and intersectional equity. Alicia's prayer speaks to the power of unmasking, not hiding our real identities, and asking God for help.

A Prayer for Those Who Refuse to Hide by Alicia T. Crosby[49]

Holy One

Give us what we need to be

For real

May we not hide our

capacity to feel or be as

we actually are

May we not hide

Our illnesses, our tears,

our neurodiversity, our complicated histories,

our exhaustion, our angst,

our apathy, our fatigue,

our questions, or even the fragments of thoughts that we bring together

with others that can make something

remarkable

And in our visibilizing what

some would want to push to

the shadows, may we take heart in

knowing that we are not alone

? Reflection Question

Exploring the intersectionality of neurodiversity with disability justice, racial justice, and LGBTQ+ justice is a beginning. There are many other forms of intersectionality that I have not included. What would you add?

CHAPTER EIGHT

The Neuroinclusive Church

**Lack of caring sees
From Powerpoint to testing
Consider with us**

 ## Neurodiversity Parable of the Postpartum Mother

After Jesus was raised from the dead, he appeared to Mary Magdalene in the garden. She asked Jesus to help show her how to best share the message of love with people who had mental health experiences that made them different.

Mary Magdalene told Jesus about the woman she had met outside the temple gates. The woman had a newborn baby strapped to her body and said the baby was hungry. The woman confessed to Mary Magdalene that she was too tired to nurse the baby and was utterly exhausted from her three days of laboring. All the mother could do was cry when the baby cried. She admitted she had not slept since the baby was born and she wasn't sure if either one of them would make it.

Mary Magdalene asked the woman, "Where are your sisters, mother, aunts, and cousins? Where is the father?"

The woman turned her head away and said, "They are all dead. And now there is no one to care about me or my baby. I am shunned by the religious authorities at the temple. They won't let me inside. I am so hungry."

Jesus listened carefully to Mary Magdalene's story and was silent for a long time. Then Jesus said, "Lack of caring sees people only as problems."

Jesus was quiet again. Then he said, "Consider with the people what is it that they need. Ask the people what they need, and they will tell you."

⌛━━ᴛ Key Words in Chapter Eight

ADA: The Americans with Disabilities Act passed in 1990 to ensure the equal rights of disabled people.

Neuroinclusive: An approach or environment that actively includes and accommodates people with diverse brain functions.

Sensory sensitivity: Sensory differences in the way a person experiences the world through their senses of taste, touch, sight, hearing, smell, and balance.

***

The Neuroinclusive Church

Blessed minds need blessed communities to grow in the love of God. We need faith communities to create ways for neurodiverse people to belong. This is where the neuroinclusive church comes in. No, this is not a separate church to which all the neurodivergent people go! A neuroinclusive church is a church that honors and celebrates the neurodivergent people who are already there, as members, volunteers, leaders, staff, and ministers. A neuroinclusive church welcomes those who have not yet stepped over the church's threshold. There are multiple creative ways faith communities can be more intentional about being a church that blesses neurodivergent minds. This is a time for us, the church, to be bold, courageous, playful, and joyful!

This chapter will tell stories about neurodiversity ministries from different congregations and share what they are trying and learning, their mistakes, and their successes. We will hear from students at Princeton Theological Seminary, a new generation of church leaders who are leading the way by developing a theology for ministries of neurodiversity. At the end of this chapter, I'll share with you my own emerging thoughts to consider as I present ten core values of a neuroinclusive ministry.

Neurodiversity Themed Worship Service

Saint George's Episcopal Church in La Cañada, California, describes itself on its website as a "liberal, progressive Episcopal Church, best known for creative worship and adult spiritual formation." The priest, Rev. Amy

Pringle, says she started exploring neurodiverse models of worship because the church rented space to organizations that support neurodiversity. It seemed a natural fit to create a worship service to serve people who frequented the campus already, people with Autism, ADHD, learning disabilities, sensory sensitivities, social anxiety, eating disorders, Down syndrome, cerebral palsy, and more.

The congregation's vision, says Rev. Amy in her welcome message on the church's website, is "not only to offer a worship service and rent a few rooms, but eventually to devote our whole 2.5-acre property to serving the neurodiverse community." Saint George's wants

> To be a place on earth where no one is the odd one out; where people and families can meet and make friends with others who experience life in similar [and different] ways; where people can feel just a little bit lighter by remembering that they're not alone; and where spiritual resources can help provide peace and hope to us all.[50]

Saint George's launched its neurodiverse worship service in February 2024. Its highlights include:

1. Short duration—planned to be 30 minutes long, though it might go longer with the interruptions, questions, and meltdowns, which are expected as a normal part of this service.

2. Soft music—no organ or other loud instruments. Based on who attends, the music might be voices-only singing, or it might be accompanied by piano or guitar. All acoustic, nothing amplified.

3. Low lighting—electric lights are dimmed or off, allowing natural light to be the primary source.

The design of the physical worship space is intentional to ensure that people do not feel crowded. The main seating area is for fewer than forty people. Additional seats, spaced farther apart, are available behind the main seating area for those who need more personal space. Everyone is asked to choose a color-coded name tag, indicating their personal space needs:

RED tags = Please don't touch me.

YELLOW tags = Please let me choose, by touching you first.

GREEN tags = No problem, it's OK to touch me.

The website's description of its neurodiverse worship service makes a point of noting that electronic devices are welcome. Guidelines for devices say to bring and use anything that helps you—but requests that users set their devices so they do not make loud noises or flash bright lights that would disturb other people. The congregation provides various accessibility aids in the sanctuary, such as fidget toys, comfort devices, reading aids, disposable earplugs, and sunglasses. Worshipers may borrow anything they like but are asked to clean items with the provided wipes after use. The church building is wheelchair accessible; signs note that the best ADA restroom is off the back hallway of the church.

I reached out to Rev. Amy by email after learning about her ministry on her website because I wanted to learn more about this vision of serving the neurodiverse community through worship and ministries. She shared with me that when they launched their first neurodiverse worship service, she was sad and surprised that no one came, despite their thorough publicity campaign. She joked about the failure to attract neurodiverse folks to a neurodiverse worship service by saying, "Go figure! No one with social anxiety was thrilled by a Grand Opening!"

Then she spent some time reflecting on why this new worship service seemed to miss the mark. Rev. Amy said, "We figured that no one wanted to pigeonhole themselves by attending a titled 'neurodiverse' service." This tracks with my discovery as well—this sense that people typically and understandably do not feel comfortable being labeled by others. The trend in disability ministry is away from specialized ministries and toward focusing on intentional belonging and inclusion for disabled people within the larger community.

Rev. Amy and her congregation took the summer to regroup and planned to relaunch the neurodiverse worship service in the fall, but this time under a different name. Instead of creating a separate worship service for neurodiversity, they decided to advertise their existing worship service as "neurodiverse-welcoming" by adding that description to their church website. They simply kept the adaptations to the worship space they had made earlier.

When I spoke with Rev. Amy she said the church had had about a dozen visitors since implementing the changes, so the plan is to watch and see how things go for a while. She said,

> [The] best part: How pleased they are to be made room for, literally and figuratively. Makes my priestly heart sing.

Second-best: The blunt honesty of neurodiverse people means they ask the questions everyone else is curious about, so even as visitors, they act as prophets for the congregation.

What Rev. Amy has learned from her efforts to make church and worship more accessible for neurodiverse folks is the difficulties of reaching people who could gain the most from it. She says,

> The worst [part] is just how incredibly hard it is and will be, to reach the people who really need major adjustments to worship (i.e., a countdown clock, visual aids, an incredibly simplified sermon/message), [to] establish trust, and [to] gather enough people in the same place at the same time to have quantum mass for a regularly scheduled special service. Herding cats seems easy by comparison.

I asked Rev. Amy about her advice to others interested in neurodiversity ministry. She says relationship-building is key:

> My advice to others is to expect to do, and do [a lot of work], maybe a full year of relationship-building before launching. Go to every parent support group, every school, every special gym, every existing group program you can find. Hang out and chat, then return and do it again. And again. And again. Get parents' input on the service. Do a soft intake process of the issues the most interested people have, and do your homework for how to address them.

Rev. Amy and her congregation created this worship for neurodivergent people with good intentions. Now she realizes that creating the worship service with and alongside the leadership of neurodivergent people and their families would be better. She says they did have disability educators volunteer to help launch the service, as well as family members of neurodivergent people. She thinks this helped, but it was not the same as having neurodiverse people themselves create and lead the worship service. She says, "All in all, I'm still learning, still experimenting, still feeling a way forward."

What we can all learn from Rev. Amy and her congregation is that nobody wants to be treated as different. That's not what neurodiversity is about. People want to be treated as equals, as valued, as respected, and as people with gifts to share. Too often churches miss the mark when we do things *for* others instead of *with* others, when we focus on being busy making our plans and we don't focus on building relationships with the very people we want to serve. Remember: "Nothing about us without us." Neurodiversity in the church needs to be relational and focus on belonging and connection to the community.

A Neuroinclusive Ministry for All Ages

One congregation creating intentional and focused ministries of neurodiversity is Abiding Presence Lutheran Church in Burke, Virginia. This church has created a neurodiverse ministry team for children, youth, and adults, which it describes as being

> For families/friends of individuals whose brains observe and navigate the world a little differently. We support each other in navigating the joys and challenges of supporting our loved ones with diagnoses that include ADHD, Autism, dyslexia, and other disabilities. We also support the whole church through discussions, training, accommodations, and resources in continuing to be a welcoming church community to neurodiverse families.[51]

This church's children's and youth ministry for Sunday school and summer camp programming is based on a workshop model. Children and youth are engaged in activities that most interest them and get to choose from a wide range of topics based on Bible stories and fun activities such as soccer, art, and Minecraft. The church staff engage in ongoing conversations with the children, youth, and caregivers to ensure that their needs are being met.

The neuroinclusive ministry for adults includes how Sunday morning worship is designed. The worship bulletin includes worship notes. For example, there is a consistent symbol used to indicate changes in the worship service or times, changes that may be overwhelming for the sensory system, such as a noisy offertory or spraying water for baptism celebrations. The sanctuary also prominently displays fidget toys for anyone to use. In addition, the church provides small group sessions for adults to discuss neurodiversity-related topics and share supportive resources.

The church also provides training about neurodiversity for all staff and volunteers. These ministries prioritize the needs of each individual and demonstrate the congregation's commitment to providing all the accommodations possible for all people to experience a sense of belonging. At the trainings, people remind one another of the church's core value:

"At Abiding Presence, we live out of our core value of 'All Are Welcome' to create a community that honors and values all brains."

Here is an example of the type of training the church provides. The goal of this training is to help members of the congregation think about how they can be more "neurodiversity-affirming" in various scenarios.

Scenario 1

You are sitting in church on Sunday with your family, and a young adult in the sanctuary is making loud noises during the service. Your daughter whispers in your ear that the young adult is old enough to know how to act in church. What do you do next?

Tips:

1. Share with your daughter that we never know what someone else's story is and that "all are welcome" in our church.

2. Reassure her that she is safe and that he is OK as well.

3. Encourage her not to stare, and explain how everyone's body may move and act differently and that's OK!

Scenario 2

One Sunday, when you turn to "pass the peace" to the family next to you, one of the children ignores your outstretched hand and looks away from you when you greet them. What do you do next?

Tips:

1. Continue greeting others in the church.

2. Remember that "all are welcome," and try not to take this minor choice personally.

3. Introduce yourself to the child and family after the service. This may lead to deeper connection opportunities where the child is more comfortable.

Scenario 3

You are at church attending a special event, and as you leave you notice a parent with their school-aged son who is lying face down on the floor crying. The parent is kneeling next to their son, talking calmly and quietly to them. What do you do next?

Tips:

1. Ask the parent, "Help or walk away?"

2. Avoid pointing, staring, or doing anything else that would draw attention to the parent and child.

3. Smile and share a "thumbs up" with the parent if they look at you.

Scenario 4

You are volunteering with a youth group event and ask a youth to read a passage from the Bible aloud. The youth says, "No, I don't want to read," while looking away from you. What do you do next?

Tips:

1. Accept their response, and move on to the next person.

2. Don't take their response personally or think poorly of the youth.

3. After the event, if appropriate, ask the youth minister and/or the youth if there are things other than reading that the youth would feel comfortable doing so that you can engage them in the future.[52]

I reached out to Rev. Meredith Lovell Keseley, senior pastor of Abiding Presence Lutheran Church, to learn more about her church's experiences developing a neuroinclusive ministry. She told the story of how the church's neuroinclusive ministry got started in the first place. She said it all began with a desire to live into their core value as a church: "all are welcome." The church made it a priority to have a children's ministry that was fully welcoming of neurodivergent children. She said, "We are committed to making church a welcoming space for nonverbal kids, 2e kids (twice-exceptional kids are gifted children who also have a disability), all kind of kids." She said, "We quickly realized families needed support, community, and safe supportive space."

Responding to the needs of families within the church, lay leaders started a neurodiversity family support group that meets once a month co-convened by two parents of neurodiverse young people, both of whom are professionals in the field. Rev. Meredith says, "Neurodiversity ministry has become a big part of who we are and how we understand our call. It all got started because I had one passionate parent willing to do something and get a group together." The seed for the neurodiversity ministry was the church's mental health team that provided support and education for the congregation. Rev. Meredith said the neurodiversity team modeled itself after their mental health team.

I asked Rev. Meredith what advice she has for congregations interested in starting a neuroinclusive ministry. She suggests finding the people in the congregation whose lives are already touched by neurodiversity. She said, "Find people who are doing this professionally. Find parents of kiddos. Find people in the community. Invite them into conversation. I have very little to do other than cheer them on. I don't bring lived experience, but I learn from them and they become the voices." Rev. Meredith is being modest about her role because, in addition to cheering on her lay leaders, she also creates new resources the church needs for its neuroinclusive ministry.

One of those self-made resources is an adapted confirmation curriculum for neurodivergent teens. She said, "This Sunday we have confirmation service for two of our neurodiverse teens. It is normally a two-hour service, but I developed confirmation materials to simplify the confirmation experience so they could have that without having stumbling blocks." Rev. Meredith said, "We write all of our own curriculum in house because we have not found anything on the market that is adaptable. I've relied heavily on professionals in the congregation in diverse fields: teaching at college level, college neurodiversity programs, special education in school."

For a congregation already deeply engaged in neuroinclusive ministry, I wondered what was on the horizon for them. Rev. Meredith said they still have more improvements to make for their sanctuary and worship experience to be more inclusive for neurodivergent folks. She said,

> One of the things we have been thinking about is how to really make worship fully welcoming space. Looking at doing some things with our physical space. Out in the narthex we have a play area for kids during worship, but we also need space for older kids, teenagers, for whom being in the sanctuary for worship may be overwhelming.

A key question driving her thoughts about neuroinclusive worship is: "How do we create worship space where neurodivergent folks can be part of the congregation but don't have to be surrounded by so many people?"

Rev. Meredith's church makes neuroinclusive ministry seem so easy. I wondered: Had she faced any barriers along the way? She says that when they first started a couple of years ago, they began with educating the congregation and there was some misunderstanding. She gave the example of electronic devices and screen time. She said,

A parent was upset about screen time among kids. But for some of our neurodiverse families screen time means something different. Screen time is a lifeline for their child when their child has to be put in overwhelming situations. There was tension between families feeling judgment around parenting when parenting a neurotypical kiddo and a neurodiverse kiddo; some days you are totally in different worlds.

The Child Mind Institute, which focuses on children's mental health advocacy, education, clinical services, and support, supports that conclusion, saying that when it comes to screen usage for neurodivergent kids, "there are benefits that are important for parents to consider as they try to manage screen time for healthy development."[53] Caroline Miller, Child Mind Institute editorial director, says the positive impact of screens on neurodivergent kids includes, "social connection, emotional grounding, and learning opportunities." Screens can also help kids "feel calmer and less anxious … offering neurodivergent children a safe and predictable space in a world that may feel overwhelming." The key takeaway is that "not all kids are alike," and that is especially true when it comes to neurodivergent kids.

The idea of neuroinclusive ministry is not the barrier: it is attitudes about inclusivity that create barriers. Consequently, the church had to navigate attitudinal barriers. Its members asked themselves, "How do we navigate families that have strong thoughts on parenting and recognize that parenting styles cannot be universal?" Rev. Meredith shared another example of ableism in the church. She said, "Someone thought the neurodivergent kids should be taught to look them in the eyes and shake their hands when they talk to them. That is lovely, but that's not how our neurodiverse kids are wired to be." The biggest challenge, she says, is how to educate the congregation.

The best teachers in the congregation, Rev. Meredith said, are the teens. She says, "Most of the resources are curriculum, and our Sunday school is taught by high school students. When we have parents teaching a class, we found that parents sometimes struggled because they felt like each child should act neurotypical. Before we switched to high schoolers teaching, we had a lot of challenges. Every high schooler has a friend who is neurodiverse. It's just understood among them."

Neurodivergent Children's Message

While it is true that there need to be more resources for churches to welcome neurodiverse people, there are already some good ones.

Congregations can draw upon the beautifully illustrated and written children's book *Next Level: A Hymn in Gratitude for Neurodiversity* by Samara Cole Doyon, published in 2024 by Tilbury House Publishers. The author is the mother of a neurodivergent son. In the opening scene of the book she describes a young boy in church for worship whose behaviors are causing a stir among some older members of the congregation. The author writes, "They can't take you in, when you're standing right here— like they're stuck in a box, trapped in some kind of fear." The illustration shows people sitting in the pew, sadly shaking their heads, looking away, and sighing. The author dedicates the book to her son, who is Autistic.

But we can overcome this feeling of being trapped in a box of fear or of our own lack of understanding, says this author:

> I want everyone to know that as the mother of a child who is visibly different, who doesn't sit still or converse in expected ways, who moves and vocalizes in his own way, and who isn't necessarily represented by nor understood in the light of the quirky, verbally blunt, mathematically ingenious type of neurodivergent characters popping up on television, it still sometimes feels like a radical act to show up with my child in the larger world, allowing and encouraging him to take up space within his own community. So often, when children like my son flap, hop, run, spin, chirp, grunt, trill, or screech in public places (stores, libraries, churches), outsiders view us as disruptions or disturbances. Children are judged as lacking discipline or morality and so are we, as parents and caregivers. As parents, we are viewed as not controlling enough, not imposing expected behaviors adequately, not forcing our children to fit into the mold required to accommodate neurotypical comfort. ... This book is a hymn of gratitude and an attempt to acknowledge and celebrate the full humanity of people who move through the world and communicate in their own unique, complete, and powerful ways.[54]

Creating a Sensory Sanctuary Resource Library

Neuroinclusive ministry can be about creating resources for people to access while they are at church. The Rev. Khaleigh Laicher of First Congregational Church of Greenwich, Connecticut, offers some suggestions on social media:

Thought I'd share something new we are doing at the First Congregational Church of Greenwich! For years now, I've dreamed of creating a space filled with sensory materials and tools for everyone to benefit from during worship. After really getting to know our church community and culture—and thanks to an incredibly generous donation—the dream started to come alive! Today, with all the pieces falling into place, I'm beyond excited to announce the launch of the "Sensory Sanctuary" Resource Library at FCCOG!

She continues:

At FCCOG, we welcome that everyone worships in unique ways, and honor the diverse needs of our community. For many, sensory items can both greatly enhance their worship experience and also provide belonging and acceptance in the worship space. That's where the Sensory Sanctuary comes in: a dedicated resource library designed to support sensory worship needs.

The Sensory Sanctuary Resource Library offers a variety of items to help create a more inclusive worship environment, including:

1. Noise-Canceling Headphones: To help reduce overwhelming sounds and create a more focused experience.

2. Fidgets: A range of tactile items such as crochet hooks and yarn, finger labyrinths, thera-putty, and more, allowing individuals to engage their hands while they worship.

3. Focusing Visual Aids: Tools that assist in maintaining attention and grounding oneself during worship.

4. Alternative Seating Options: Rocking chairs, catering to individual preferences and needs.

The Sensory Sanctuary is part of our ongoing commitment to providing the tools and resources that everyone deserves to make the Meetinghouse accessible and welcoming for all. We already do this through offerings like auditory aids and closed captioning, ramps and the Liftovator, and now, also through sensory implementations. Located at the back of the Meetinghouse, the Sensory Sanctuary Resource Library is available for all worshippers. We invite you to explore these resources and enrich your worship experience in a space that values and embraces diversity. No matter who you are, where you are on life's journey, or your sensory requirements, you are welcome at First Church.

I reached out to Rev. Khaleigh through social media to thank her for her neuroinclusive ministry. She replied, "I'm just trying to live out my faith how I think God has asked me to." She shared about her motivation for creating a neuroinclusive ministry: "This has been a dream of mine for years, but was made reality with a donation. The donation was specifically for me to 'get creative'! After being in my church for a year, and getting to know the families of my congregation, I felt like it could be a good fit."

I asked Rev. Khaleigh what had surprised her and challenged her so far in the creation and implementation of neuroinclusive ministries. She shared she is surprised by "just how many people loved the idea, how many people came to me and told me about their neurodivergent loved ones, and how the tools in the Sensory Sanctuary engaged neurotypical children in worship as well." She said the biggest challenge so far is educating the congregation. "Those who are familiar with sensory needs in the neurodivergent community immediately understood the purpose of the space. But to many this was new language and a learning opportunity."

For folks interested in starting a neuroinclusive ministry, she says it has worked well to be casual in her approach. She says she is "confident in my communication, and modeling and engaging with the tools myself." The most important thing about getting started is to "find a support team of staff and parents to walk this journey with you!"

An Extravagant Welcome and Neurodiversity

Galileo Church in Fort Worth, Texas, is another example of a congregation that celebrates neurodiversity. The church's motto is: "We do kindness around mental illness and mental health, and we celebrate neurodiversity." How does Galileo Church express its desire to be a neuro-informed congregation? This is what it says to people curious and wanting to know more about the church:

Please don't wait to be "normal" or "well" before you come to church. We're ready to receive you with your sadness, or your social anxiety, or your unnamable, undiagnosed quirkiness.

Lots of us have been there, or are there, or know somebody there. Compassion, transparency, and empowerment are the gifts we can offer. We are especially loving toward kids who are looking for friends who will love them just as they are.[55]

Galileo Church's ministries are designed to accommodate and support neurodiversity. The church has created a "quiet room" located in the back of the worship space and encourages people to feel free to move around. The church advertises on its website that the

> Quiet room has a "sensory library" (think sensory café, but you can check out the materials and take them with you if you want/need). It's stocked with weighted blankets, hammocks/hanging chairs, a stationary bike, fidget toys, earplugs, noise-canceling headphones, and etc. ... It's *for you*.

In explaining more about their neurodiversity informed church, the church says,

> It's honestly a little hard to say how our church practices this particular kindness. You sort of know it when you see it, right? For example, every Sunday we announce at the top of our worship service, "We've planned a liturgy for tonight ... but if what we've planned isn't working for you, if you need to do something else during this hour, you've got total freedom to do that. Pace in the back; go outside for a cig; or find some respite in the Quiet Room at the back of the worship space."

In its own words, here are other ways Galileo celebrates neurodiversity:

1. We try not to hug without asking.

2. We never make participation in what we're doing compulsory.

3. We let kids and adults alike tell us what's best for them, and we trust people when they say something is bad for them.

4. And we encourage story-telling, the narration of your very own life, from the perspective of mental illness—depression, anxiety, whatever you've got—and/or the perspective of neurodiversity—Autism, bring it on.

The church's website states: "We're all doing our best with the brains God gave us, and helping each other get the most out of this sometimes beautiful, sometimes painful, always complicated life."

I reached out to Galileo Church's pastor, Rev. Katie Hays, for conversation about her church's neuroinclusive ministries. I told her how helpful I found her church's website. She said,

> Neurodivergent people shouldn't have to guess, let's just be explicit as possible on their website. A fear churches might have is that if they advertise, then they might be "overrun" by people with these disabilities. I get that. But the stuff neurodiverse people are asking for is not hard, and it's not expensive and is good practice.

Galileo began as a new church start and is now over eleven years old. Neurodiversity was not a ministry priority for the congregation when the church was first formed. Rev. Katie said they developed their neuroinclusive ministry "sort of accidentally, or [through the] Holy Spirit." The ministry grew organically in response to the conversations people were having in her church about mental health. Especially given the political and cultural environment in Texas, their original missional priority was justice for LGBTQ+ folks. She said the church wanted "to make a space where queer people and allies could be the same person on Sunday as they were the other days of the week."

The church created a safe space where people could come out as part of the LGBTQ+ community and be transparent about their gender identities and sexual orientations. But then something unexpected happened. "When you invite people to be transparent about their identity, you get a lot more transparencies," Rev. Katie reported. People also started becoming transparent about their mental health and identifying as neurodivergent.

Rev. Katie says this is a generational shift she sees in the church. Unlike prior generations who masked mental health realities and neurodiversity on account of the associated stigma and shame, younger generations are different. She said,

> People younger than Gen X were talking a lot more about mental health, their medications, their appointments, their diagnoses, and referrals. We had a lot of young millennials ten years ago in the first wave of Autism and ADHD diagnoses. They were developing ways to talk about it as adults.

Efforts to break the silence and to end the stigma and shame of mental health symptoms and diagnoses are making a positive difference.

The church's neuroinclusive ministry was born out of an effort to "adapt to make worship and friendship accessible and celebratory of how people show up in the space." Rev. Katie tells the story about one family with seven children who visited the church for the first time. The mother told Rev. Katie they were looking for a church that accepted all her children, including her three children with Down syndrome. A heartbreaking, yet all too common, story unfolded. The mother told Rev. Katie the story about her three disabled children who were not able to pass the confirmation class offered at their church, so the disabled children were denied the sacrament of holy communion. As Rev. Katie told me this story, her voice became firm as she said, "At our church, not only could they *take* communion, but they could *serve* communion."

As Rev. Katie told me about her church's neuroinclusive ministry, she shared that she had learned some important things from her daughter's school and how the people there accommodated neurodivergent students. Rev. Katie recounted, "My older daughter is Autistic, and we got the diagnoses at a time twenty-five years ago when not many girls were getting those diagnoses, so our whole family [had to] adjust." Her daughter's school got a grant to help create a sensory resource center at the school. This helped her daughter and other students navigate the learning environment successfully. And one of her daughter's favorite activities was using the stationary bicycle. About the school sensory space, Rev. Katie says, "They had a menu that had options like 'things to wake you up' and 'things to calm you down.' The kids learned to self-regulate by choosing from the menu what they needed to do. Each person gets to decide what they need."

Rev. Katie reminds us that there are many families like hers and that, as society becomes more open to talking about mental health and neurodiversity, culture and society are changing. She said,

Normalizing conversations is key. Normalize that parents can say, "I have an IEP [Individual Education Program] meeting tomorrow. I'm stressed. Can you pray [for me]?" It's hard as a parent, so maybe the pastor can go [with them] for support. All clergy should get way more educated about how to help parents, families, and individuals [make it] through the school systems. We can go to the school and work systems to help advocate for people in systems that are not always kind. It's such an important part of their well-being.

I wondered how a church might begin to take small steps to create a neuroinclusive ministry based on what Rev. Katie has seen work at Galileo. She suggested one start with making simple changes, such as the music in worship. She said, "Our music is soft. It's one woman on an acoustic guitar, and it's soothing. It turns out a lot of us appreciate that." Other simple steps a church of any size can do is to focus on the worship setting. She said, "The setting really matters. Lighting matters. The sound matters." A space that is too big will make bouncy sounds, and a space that is too bright will be triggering for folks with light sensitivity. One idea she has for large spaces is to install decorative panels that are sound-absorbent. As to the lighting, she said, "We have low lighting on Sundays, and we can adjust the lighting up and down for the sake of a sense of calm and focus. It helps folks with Attention Deficit Disorder (ADD), as well, to lessen the stimulation in the space."

In addition to the changes in the sanctuary, churches can create parallel spaces where people can still be part of worship but have a less sensory-stimulating experience. Galileo has a "quiet room." Rev. Katie reports, "We make a promise that in the quiet room, though you may not be alone, it will be quiet. A soft place to land with chairs, a little desk. The room is here, and it is a promise. Whether the room gets used or not, it's a promise that you will be OK."

At the beginning of every worship service, a worship leader announces that people have permission to move around the space, to walk around the back, to pace, and to stim. The back wall of the sanctuary has a sensory library, a shelving unit of four shelves that is seven feet tall. Rev. Katie said, "The sensory library includes bouncy balls, bean bags, weighted blankets, fidgets, and a lightweight sensory bike; this gets used every Sunday. It provides a gross motor (big muscle movement) reset." Her own family's experience with neurodiversity that began over fifteen years ago with the sensory resource center at her daughter's school inspired this sensory library for her church. One of the reasons she likes the church's sensory library is because "it gives people a chance to try the sensory stuff out to see if they like it." I asked her who is in charge of it, and she said, for example: "Over the summer, a cohort of neurodiverse adults met to replenish the library. One of the bins was filled with 1,000 pipe cleaners. They all got used up. So the team is going to replenish the pipe cleaners."

Simple changes to the worship service itself can be more neuroinclusive, such as offering multiple ways to pray and different ways to engage in faith formation. Rev. Katie described her church's use of body prayer in the worship service:

> We use multi-sensory body prayer in worship. We use bad yoga, bad mime, and bad sign language to pray. We invite people to move their bodies and pause to prayer. Something as simple as turning their heads gently in one direction and then pausing. If we engage the body and muscles, people [manage to] stay with us as we pray.

In addition to the style of the worship service, for faith formation for children and teens the church offers two options for families to choose from, depending on what works best for their child, regardless of age. She said,

> We have a kids' group and youth group but there is no age cut-off. We have activity-based learning (that's the kids' group), and we have a discussion-based learning (that's the youth group). A person with a developmental disability might prefer the kids' group, and an Autistic child might like the discussion-based youth group.

Now the church embraces neuroinclusive ministry as a core part of their mission. They have flags around the walls of their sanctuary—a pride flag, a Black Lives Matter flag, and the neurodiversity flag, a rainbow infinity symbol.

In addition to creating a culture of inclusion for neurodivergent folks, they are working on creating a culture of belonging. This part is more complex. Rev. Katie describes the tension between the neurofamilies whose children feel comfortable expressing themselves and moving around the sanctuary during worship and the neurodivergent adults who may prefer more stillness and quiet. Now, she is discerning with her church leaders whether all these accommodations can be met at the same time and in the same space.

> Families with neurodiverse kids have told me that they love our space. It's a barn. They said, "If my kid is running wild, melting down, overstimulating, or just excited to be here, there's so little chance they will break something. I don't have to worry." It lets family relax and breathe a sigh of relief.

At the same time, Rev. Katie reflects, this high-energy dynamic can be disturbing to folks who prefer a calm worship environment.

How can we accommodate the activities of the kids when it overstimulates the neurodiverse adults who ask us to "settle those kids down." And I have Jesus who says, "Let the little kids come to me." How do we do both (really good things) in consideration with each other?

One idea they are working on together is to do a space usage audit, "to look at the space and how we can use it to make it work for everyone." As a core value of the church, they are determined to find a way to work together to accommodate everyone. That is what the neurodivergent Body of Christ looks like in action.

We wrapped up our conversation dreaming about the future of the church and the role of neuroinclusive ministries in congregations. Rev. Katie reminded me: "Kids with diagnoses are going to become adults with diagnoses. They are going to need spiritual resources. If workplaces can figure it out, then the church surely can do it! If the Holy Spirit is calling us to do this, then we'd better catch up."

How to Foster a Welcoming, Neurodiverse Church

Rev. Jess Harron is a disability advocate and pastor of a local church. As someone with multiple disabilities herself, she helps to educate congregations about accessibility and inclusion ministries. In her blog post "How to Welcome Those With Disabilities in Church," she suggests several ways churches can be more welcoming. Here are Rev. Jess' suggestions for being more welcoming of neurodiversity:

1. **People with disabilities and/or neurodivergent people might not want to be cured. How one preaches on Bible stories matters. Jesus is unlikely to cure my DNA. However, Jesus brings me great healing.** Learn the difference between healing and cure. Preach about how healing in the Bible might have included a physical cure but was mostly about restoration to community and breaking down barriers. Consider asking a disabled person to preach (and pay them) whenever healing texts come up [in the Lectionary].

2. **For neurodivergent people, things like sitting still, paying attention, bright lights, and loud music might be difficult to handle. There might be some days people can manage it and some days they cannot.** If someone asks to have the music turned down, do it. Provide a quieter, darker space in a corner of the sanctuary. Provide a little tent with a bean bag chair. Keep

your thoughts to yourself if someone is wearing sunglasses or hearing protection in church. Provide a sensory swing or personal workout trampoline. Have a quiet room, like the library, where sound and video can come in and Autistic people or those with post-traumatic stress disorder (PTSD) or social anxiety can go to re-regulate themselves. Have a small group go through your worship from entering the front door to leaving and record every sensory input they experience on a Sunday. [Ask them to note] every sound, sight, touch, taste, smell, and physical input [they] experience. Learn from that and provide options. For example, can there be a darker place in the sanctuary? Can things be hung that dampen echoes in fellowship halls? How many textures of seating do you offer?

3. **There are many reasons some people do not like to be touched. For some it causes pain, for some it increases anxiety, for some it brings up traumatic memories, for some it leads to ... sensory overload. Please understand that even if you are a "hugging church," consent matters. My reality is that some days I can be touched and some days I cannot. I normally love to hug but on my high pain days I do not. Just because I consent to a hug one week does not mean I will do it the next.** During the sharing of the peace when I am the pastor, I say "In a moment we will share the peace with each other. Please do this with respect for consent and always ask before giving a handshake or hug. If someone [simply] waves at you, please wave back."

4. **I wish you would take the time and energy to learn more about people with disabilities. (For example, did you know that some communities prefer person-first language and some identity-first language? Do you know what the people in your community prefer?)** Read stories, follow blogs, follow on social media, and listen to podcasts by people with disabilities. For example, EDS TikTok is amazing [educational videos about Ehlers-Danlos Syndrome]. Be sure to include those with mobility issues, deaf people, and people who are blind. Follow Autistic people and learn from them (many Autistic people do not consider Autism to be a disability.)

5. **You can do this!** Although helping your church be a welcoming place for people with disabilities can be challenging work, it

can also be rewarding. You are learning to love your neighbor as yourself; this is what Jesus asks us to do. You can do this. I know it might seem overwhelming, especially if you have not thought about it before or are not close to someone who is open about their disabilities. (I guarantee you know disabled people. They might have invisible disabilities, they might never talk about them, or they might have determined not to talk to you about them based on the language you use.) You are not expected to do everything on this list. Not everything can be for everyone for all time. If you are in a 100-year-old church building with one hundred stairs, unless you are sitting on millions of dollars, I do not expect you to make your church accessible for me. (Elevators and bathroom remodels are expensive.) It is OK if you do not have the resources to do all of these things. Pick two to three things you *can* do in your congregation. Many of you can read a book or fill your social media feeds with authors and creators who are Autistic or disabled. There are small everyday changes that each of us can do to help the church and the world be a less ableist place and more welcoming for all of us.[56]

Neurodiversity Theology and Ministry

Disability, mental health, and neurodiversity are being discussed by theological education students around the lunch tables. Maci Sepp, who currently serves as director of vocational outreach at Columbia Theological Seminary, leads one of these conversations. When she was a master of divinity student at Princeton Theological Seminary, she reflected theologically on ministries that honored and celebrated neurodiversity in the church. These reflections led to essays that provided theological insights into why neurodiversity is important for the church. The collection is part of the Theology and Neurodiversity Project.[57]

According to Maci, fear is one of the key obstacles to churches developing accessible ministries for neurodivergent people. She saw fear in action at one of the churches she visited for her research—fear of making a mistake, fear of not knowing what to do, fear of being wrong, and fear of looking foolish. Stigma and shame are barriers not only for disabled and neurodivergent people, but also for people wanting to create inclusive ministries. These feelings of overwhelm and anxiety often prevent anything happening to create positive change.

Continuing her research, Maci visited a church known for its neurodiversity ministry. Maci asked them how they ministered to neurodivergent people. The answer was simple. Maci said, "It began with the basic question of asking their neurodivergent congregants, congregants with disabilities, and their families what they needed." Nothing about neurodiversity without involving people with neurodiversity, right? Even though this simple approach is so basic, we often overlook it. Disabled people are often not included in planning disability ministries because ableism tries to erase their wisdom and expertise.

By beginning the neurodiversity ministry in relationships with neurodiverse children, youth, families, and adults, the congregation had a solid foundation on which to build. Guided by neurodiverse folks in the church, they made changes such as adapting worship services, adding new programs, and increasing awareness about disability and neurodiversity in the day-to-day life of the congregation. Maci said the church's neurodiversity ministries were blessed because "others from outside the church community started hearing about the changes that were happening and decided to flock to them."

As Maci reflects on the church, she says what she found was hopeful. "I am encouraged to know that being more inclusive and helping people belong can start with such a simple question. I am also delighted to see what the power of recognition—of noticing someone and asking them what they need—has the potential to do." In a way, this is how Jesus moved in the world. Jesus noticed people right where they were and engaged in conversations about what they needed right then.

Maci says she finds hope even when stigma and shame hinders the Spirit's movement to bring change to the church. She says she finds it hopeful that

> The reason that changes are not happening is not necessarily because of a lack of compassion. My greatest fear is that churches are indifferent, but listening to my friend and others in ministry I realize that there is still a significant amount of empathy. Their biggest hurdle is not a mountain of indifference; rather, people just do not know where to begin.

This is the good news. We can overcome the fear, stigma, and shame preventing ministries of neurodiversity by helping to break the silence. We can begin with one conversation at a time.

One of the most important elements of disability ministry in the church is to understand that our churches already have disabled and neurodivergent people in them. When we make changes to better accommodate disabled and neurodivergent folks, we make improvements for everyone's benefit, including those who are already there. This is the theory of universal design. Maci said, "Much of what I have learned from the past semester is that many of the changes and accommodations made on behalf of neurodivergent people can improve the learning of all participants, no matter their neurobiology."

Here is a summary of what Maci suggests faith communities can do, not only to create neurodiverse ministries, but to create a sense of belonging for everyone:

1. Print bulletins with bigger sans-serif fonts [which are easier to read], and color coding; and incorporate images alongside the text;

2. Have both audio and video versions of Bible stories to use in Sunday school;

3. Provide written and auditory worship instructions;

4. Never assume that people know when to sit or stand, speak or be silent, move around or stay in their pews;

5. Preach about learning disabilities from the pulpit; and

6. Continually evaluate changes by a group consisting of the church leadership and people with learning disabilities every step of the way, asking what is missing, what could be improved, and what needs to be taken out completely.

Calling the Church to Use More Expansive and Evolving Language

I serve on the national staff of the United Church of Christ as the minister for disability and mental health justice. In addition to supporting the United Church of Christ Disabilities Ministries Board, I support the work of the United Church of Christ Mental Health Network. I've been connected with the Mental Health Network for over fifteen years, first as a volunteer board member and now as a staff member. During this time we have created resources and programs to support congregations in creating innovative mental health ministries. We developed a curriculum called WISE (Welcoming, Inclusive, Supportive, and Engaged)[58] for mental health. The UCC has been dedicated to mental health ministries going back to the 1980s and to disabilities ministries even earlier.

Most recently, the Mental Health Network has begun to move in the direction of embracing more inclusive language for mental health. They are leading the way in faith-based mental health ministry and are urging UCC bodies at all levels to update language regarding those living with mental health experiences and neurodiversity in a way that reduces stigma and encourages inclusivity. They are inviting us to understand the harm and offense many people feel when language is used that does not affirm their individual and/or collective identities. In the spirit of love, the Mental Health Network encourages us all to use language that honors the diversity of blessed minds.

I am encouraged by ministries like the Mental Health Network, which is leading the way to promote the use of non-stigmatizing language. Language that avoids creating the "other" promotes mental health and well-being. Language is ever-evolving and may change as society changes and may differ based on context. I thank God for faith communities that recognize, proclaim, and celebrate the basic sacred right each individual has to their own mental health.

Neuroinclusive Ministry

Whether you are part of a larger network of congregations, already have a mental health and/or disability ministry or don't have one yet, every church can work on becoming more inclusive of neurodiversity. Churches can be more intentional about improving accessibility by creating what I am calling "neuroinclusive ministry." Neuroinclusive ministry includes anyone experiencing brain differences. It is important for neurodiverse-informed ministry to be inspired by the desire to share God's love. The reason we are creating welcoming, inclusive, supportive, and engaging neurodiverse faith communities is to follow the teachings of Jesus to love our neurodiverse neighbors and our neurodiverse selves.

As we create new models for neuroinclusive ministries, we want to be guided by best practices. According to research in the academic field of neurodiversity studies, there are five recommended areas for awareness and consideration related to neurodiversity. This list can help shape how a church or ministry will address the following needs for accommodations and support:[59]

1. Managing day-to-day activities

2. Adapting to changes in routines

3. Navigating social interactions

4. Sensory demands

5. Barriers posed by disability related bias or social stigma

Reflection Question

How do these five areas affect the way you think about and design a neuroinclusive ministry? Which area do you perceive to be the easiest and which the most challenging to tackle? How might you adapt an existing ministry or activity, such as worship, so that it better addresses these five areas? Is there anything you would add to the list?

Ten Core Values for Neuroinclusive Ministry

As you consider practical ways to update your own congregation's ministries and other settings of ministry, such as campus ministry, I invite you to adopt a set of core values to guide your actions. Here are ten core values for a neuroinclusive ministry setting that I have distilled from other leaders' efforts and my own:

1. Each mind is blessed. Neurodiversity is not a problem to be solved, but a blessing.

2. No ministry benefits from making assumptions about people's identities and what people need. The realities, identities, needs, and accommodations of each unique person are honored, respected, and considered.

3. "Nothing about us without us." Neurodivergent people and their loved ones are involved in the planning, formation, and leadership of the ministry.

4. The context for ministry is grounded in creating healthy boundaries around physical spaces, physical touch, sensitivity to sensory stimulation such as sound and light, clear guidelines and scheduling, and options honoring each person's sense of personal well-being, including freedom of movement.

5. Accommodations are provided with grace and joy, offering multiple and ongoing opportunities for accessibility needs to be expressed and met.

6. The highest priority is given to building relationships of trust, compassion, and mutual care that create a sense of community.

7. Communication is open and clear, incorporating various forms of written, verbal, and visual communication, as well as an openness to communicating in ways that best meet the needs of individuals.

8. Flexibility is valued and change is encouraged to allow for adaptations based on feedback and responses to emerging needs.

9. The goal is belonging, not just inclusion. Inclusion is what makes it possible for people to be there. Belonging means that you want them there, that they are active members, and that they will be missed if they are not there.

10. The guiding spiritual purpose is sharing the radically powerful and hopeful love of God. This purpose shapes every aspect of ministry. There is no judgment, stigma, or shame allowed.

These ten core values can root your neuroinclusive ministry and help connect you to the neurodiversity movement in the church.

? Reflection Question

What is missing from the list of ten values? What would you change, adapt, delete, or add? The beauty of neuroinclusive ministry is that by design it can be adapted to fit your specific context and needs. Just as no blessed mind is exactly the same as another, so too no neurodiverse ministry setting will be exactly the same as another. Diversity is a divine gift from God.

∞ Story Illustration

After over a decade of not having a youth group, last year we started one at my church where I serve as the pastor. Surprisingly, it was not organized by our Christian Education team. Our youth group was started by our mental health team. We wanted to create a youth group experience that prioritized the mental well-being and mind/body/spirit connection of our youth. The first priority for our youth ministry was honoring the blessed minds of our youth.

We meet in the basement area that is our large fellowship hall. To prepare the space, we set out on the tables fidget toys and the "calming jars" we created as a youth group activity. Calming jars were a simple craft made from plastic jars, clear Elmer's glue, colorful food-dye drops, and glitter. We also created a "cozy corner" in the corner of the large room with comfy chairs, blankets, and low lighting. It's a safe space in the same room as the group, but a quieter area for someone to take time to regroup, get regulated, and recover from overstimulation. The youth help put it together, and all the items were donated by church members. It's decorated with artwork from the youth that we made together as an activity session.

When we first began meeting with the youth group, we invited the youth to help create a group covenant. We spent one of our first sessions together discussing and writing this covenant. We read it at the beginning of every gathering as we circle around a candle.

Reading the youth group covenant, we pledge to:[60]

1. Respect others and accept their boundaries

2. Respect others' physical space and right to be alone

3. Respect others' neurodivergence

4. Listen to others without interruption while they are speaking

5. Care for the building and share space equitably with other groups who may be here

6. Ask for clarification/explanation when you need it or when you don't understand

7. Use phones only during break time, emergencies, and special circumstances

8. Follow this covenant

This group covenant has enabled neurodivergent youth to feel seen, honored, and respected and has created an environment to form deeper connections.

Every youth group gathering includes sharing a meal together. During our mealtime, usually pizza, we go around the table and share in a time of mental health check-ins. We call this "high, low, disco." Each person, youth and adult, has an opportunity to speak freely about the best part of their week (high), the worst part of their week (low), and a random thought or idea or thing they want to share (disco). This time of connection is sacred. Even though we don't read from the Bible in youth group, we share the Gospel through telling the stories of our lives, opening our hearts to one another and to God.

Through creating emotionally supportive spiritual community, we are reaching youth with the power of God's love. Neuroinclusive youth ministry happens when neurodivergent youth are supported and accommodated and the teachings of Jesus are shared in the church's actions. "They will know we are Christians by our love" is not just a song lyric, it is at the heart of neuroinclusive ministry. After a year of building trust with our youth group, now in our second year, we are being invited to explore possible partnerships with a local high school's neurodiversity club because one of our teens is now a leader of the school's club. We are a small church. Yet with God's help, we can make a big difference in a teen's life. It's amazing what the Neurodivergent God is doing in and through the church!

? Reflection Question

What does it mean to you that the Body of Christ is neurodivergent? Which of these neuroinclusive ministry examples most excites you? What is one step you could take to begin to experiment with creating a neuroinclusive ministry?

CHAPTER NINE

The Neurodivergent Minister

**God calls me to be
My neurodivergent self
God blesses my mind**

 ### Neurodiversity Parable of Neurodivergent Jesus' Call to Ministry

When Jesus was a young child, one of his favorite things to do was to explore the countryside and talk to God. It was there, under the big sky, that Jesus lost track of time and was happiest. But Jesus' parents worried about him. He would disappear, and they did not know where he had gone.

Jesus often heard a voice calling to him. One day this voice led Jesus to the synagogue, where the rabbi was reading from the scroll of the prophet Isaiah, "The Spirit of God is upon me because God has anointed me to proclaim good news to the poor." Jesus wondered whether this was the same Spirit of God that was upon him during his own adventures in the wilderness.

Jesus pondered this in his heart: "Is God calling me to devote my life to God and become a rabbi?" Jesus' heart raced, and he worried about what he was supposed to do with his life. He kept his fears to himself. He felt different from other children his age. He preferred the company of adults. Jesus was different.

Key Words in Chapter Nine

ADHD: Attention Deficit Hyperactivity Disorder is a neurological disability affecting one's ability to focus and/or can manifest as impulsive behaviors.

Bipolar: A mental health diagnosis characterized by extreme shifts in mood, energy, and activity.

Neurofamily: A family in which one or more members is/are neurodivergent.

***

The Neurodivergent Minister

When you have met one neurodivergent minister, you have met one neurodivergent minister. Each person has their own unique stories, identities, and experiences of their sense of calling as a neurodivergent minister. In this chapter we will hear multiple stories and reflections about the experiences of being a neurodivergent minister. (What stories would you add?) If a neurodivergent minister has a family and one or more of the family members are also neurodivergent, this is called a neurofamily, so we have some stories about that, too. I hope these stories will help the congregations calling neurodivergent ministers to partner with them, and help the church better understand the unique gifts and opportunities neurodivergent ministers bring to the church.

To my knowledge there is no specific data available yet about the percentage of ministers who identify as neurodivergent. However, using three factors we can make an educated guess based on the data we do have. First, the rate of mental health experiences and diagnoses among ministers. According to the Duke Divinity School's Clergy Health Initiative, ministers of local churches experience higher rates of symptoms of depression than nonclergy.[61] Second, research shows that 16 percent of ministers reported having symptoms of anxiety. And third, in the general public, one in four people is disabled, so we can conclude about the same statistic, if not higher, for ministers given their higher rates of depression than the nonclergy public. Thus, we can make an educated guess that at least 20 percent of ministers are neurodivergent. This gives us an estimate from which to work, though more research is needed.

 ### Reflection Question

If neurodiversity among ministers is more common than we realize, then how might the church respond better to accommodate the needs of neurodivergent ministers? What are the lived experiences of neurodivergent ministers, and what can we learn from their stories?

Autism Pastor

This conversation about neurodivergent ministers is possible because of the faithful groundwork of the Autistic community, both outside and inside the church. Take, for example, Lamar Hardwick, who is author of the book *Disability and the Church: A Vision for Diversity and Inclusion*.[62] Rev. Lamar was diagnosed with Autism as an adult and while serving in ministry as pastor of a local church. He writes about what it was like for him to learn that he was Autistic:

> When I was first diagnosed with Autism, I was both relieved and grieved all at the same time. For thirty-six years I had lived life without a working knowledge of who I was, how my brain was wired, or any semblance of self-worth and identity as a person or as a Christian. When I was diagnosed, it was like meeting myself for the first time. I wasn't grieving that I had Autism, but truthfully I grieved all the lost opportunities from my past. I wasn't fearful for my future[;] after all, I had managed to do pretty well up until that point. What I grieved was the life that I'd never had because I had a limited understanding of why things were working as they had.[63]

Rev. Lamar also experiences the intersectionality of disability, race, and religion as a Black Autistic pastor. Tied to this reality, he heeded the call to write *How Ableism Fuels Racism* to help Christian communities engage in critical conversations about race by addressing issues of ableism. Hardwick believes ableism—the idea that certain bodies are better than others—and the disability discrimination fueled by this perspective are the root causes of racial bias and injustice in American culture and in the church. He uses historical records, biblical interpretation, and disability studies to examine how ableism in America led to the creation of images, idols, and institutions that perpetuate both disability and racial discrimination.

He then goes a step further, calling the church into action to address the deep-seated issues of ableism that started it all and offering practical steps to help readers dismantle ableism and racism both in attitude and in practice.[64] In his other book he writes, "Ableism could be considered the social equivalent of racism. To understand ableism we must see it in terms not of individual behavior or disdain toward the disabled but as a social structure and system that marginalizes people with disabilities."[65]

Rev. Lamar self-identifies publicly as "Autism Pastor" on his social media sites. He explained why:

God's image is reflected in all of creation, and the church should seek to bring attention to the very image of God that is seen in the lives of those who live with disability. I believe that what the disability community most needs from the church in order to feel welcomed and valued is a church that intentionally includes them in being image bearers of God. This is the primary reason for the mission of diversity.[66]

Rev. Lamar notably does not use the word "neurodivergent" in his book. Yet his work on disability and the church helps us better understand the experience of neurodivergent clergy and specifically what it is like for him to be an Autistic pastor.

For Rev. Lamar, learning he was Autistic prompted deep personal reflection and growth. Though it was also a time of change and grief, his diagnosis also prompted joy given his congregation's response. Rev. Lamar shares:

After disclosing my Autism diagnosis to my congregation in 2015, we began to see an increase in families attending that had children with developmental disabilities or mental health issues. We also began to see an increase in our existing attendees feeling more comfortable in disclosing issues they had been struggling with silently. Families who had children diagnosed with Autism, anxiety disorders, ADHD, and various other intellectual and developmental disabilities all began reaching out to me and to our church. Each family from our community came with a unique story about how disability and stigma had kept them from regular church attendance.[67]

Rev. Lamar's story highlights how a person's neurodiversity can lead to deeper relationships. Neurodivergent ministers help the church become more like the neurodivergent Body of Christ. This is especially important because people and families with neurodiversity are less likely to go to church. Indeed, Rev. Lamar discovered in his research that the church is not as inclusive as it thinks.

Reflection Question

Why would neurodivergent people have a lower chance of attending church? What barriers to accessibility we are not addressing as a church?

Repeatedly, the most challenging barriers to inclusivity and belonging for neurodivergent folks are stigma and judgmental attitudes. In the foreword to Rev. Lamar's book, Bill Gaventa, author, speaker, and consultant specializing in the intersection of disability and spirituality, writes:

> At the heart of discussions about both diversity and disability are the emotional fears and attitudinal sins of stigma and prejudice of the "other" that solidify into systemic discrimination and social barriers. At the heart is our collective failure to see and honor the image of God in every single person whom God has created, or in secular terms, to see that we are created equal with the right to life, liberty, and happiness, as well as our collective failure to enjoy, marvel at, and celebrate the diversity of humankind as a foundation of God's creation.[68]

Rev. Lamar offers this encouragement to neurodivergent and disabled people who want to pastor a church:

> People with disabilities have always been successful when given the right opportunities. Pastoring a church for me requires certain accommodations that make pursuing my calling possible. I need special assistance with scheduling, note taking in meetings, and social events. When certain accommodations are put in place, it increases my effectiveness because I don't have to spend time on tasks that are challenging for me because of Autism. The plan has worked well for me, but it is truly because of the people who have committed to a relationship with me, serving alongside me, and helping me to pursue the calling that God has placed on my life to pastor. It is not always easy, but the relationships are most important and most affirming.[69]

As an Autistic pastor, Rev. Lamar notes the four top characteristics of churches that create ministries of disability inclusion. Congregational disability inclusion ministries do the following:[70]

1. Put people over programs, and have an attitude of inclusion that will make things happen, realizing that it's not all about the programs and resources

2. Celebrate rather than tolerate differences as gifts from God, realizing that all persons are made in God's image

3. Give preference to circles over rows (e.g., in meetings and educational settings) to emphasize building relationships among equals

4. Have a faith leader or pastor for whom inclusion is a priority of their ministry

A Neurodivergent Minister with ADHD

The Rev. Kay Rohloff is a minister who was diagnosed with ADHD as an adult. She describes her diagnosis and her neurodivergence as a gift. In her blog post "Your ADHD Pastor and You," she highlights that ministers who are neurodivergent bring with them unique gifts.

> Since our brains work a little differently, we often make connections others don't. This might appear at work as creativity, a knack for problem-solving, or surprising moments of intuition and insight. We can also manage emergency situations very well, whether they are medical emergencies, or suddenly needing to lead a class at the last minute. (This is exhausting, so please don't feel the need to create these situations for us!) You'll find we have great resilience about everyday life. Our ability to jump from task to task also helps us bounce back from setbacks.[71]

Rev. Kay wants churches to know that ministers who are neurodivergent may live with multiple mental health experiences, like anxiety and depression. She recommends churches not be surprised if their neurodivergent ministers have therapists and choose not to drink alcohol. These may be important ways they are managing their well-being.

She offers congregations tips for supporting ministers who are neurodivergent—specifically, those who have ADHD like her. She says:

1. If you want us to remember something, *write it down*. Times that by ten for Sunday morning! (We also love written meeting agendas, as well as presentations with handouts.)

2. Encourage us to have scheduled time to work in the office *without interruptions*. This may mean having specific "drop in" hours once or twice a week. (Make sure any other church staff honor the no-interruptions rule too!)

3. Be especially clear about punctuality expectations with us. If the event starts at eight, but you want *us* there at 7:30, tell us that as soon as you can. (By writing it down, of course!)

Rev. Kay also encourages churches to support ministers as they navigate what coping methods work best for them. For example, time management support means honoring their request for extra time to get prepared and organized before a meeting. Congregations can support neurodivergent ministers in caring for their own physical health through making time for meals, limiting evening meetings to no more than twice a week, as well as holding them accountable for using up all their allotted vacation time.

She jokes that churches should make sure there's plenty of strong coffee because caffeine helps people with ADHD focus. "Don't be surprised if we take our caffeine very seriously indeed!" Perhaps instead of a "Buy your pastor a beer day" we need a "Buy your pastor a coffee day!" I reached out to Rev. Kay, and she shared with me in a social media message: "So far no one has had a problem with me taking coffee very seriously."

I asked Rev. Kay what advice she would give to people who are neurodivergent and preparing for ministry. She said,

> Well, my major problem in seminary was that I didn't know I was neurodivergent, so if there's any one comment I would make, it's that I wish seminaries would do a little education on some of the more likely diagnoses. Especially for how they present in people who are not white male. If I had known about my ADHD at any given time, it would have saved me several giant messes in my life, including the loss of my first call.

Rev. Kay is now providing the resources for others that she herself wishes she had had. She spoke on a podcast episode about professional women with ADHD called "Women and ADHD" hosted by Katy Weber. "I talked about how being a pastor, especially a pastor of a smaller church, can be really suitable for someone with ADHD because we get to set our own schedule and be very flexible about things."

Not only can ministry be a good vocational fit for neurodivergent folks, but folks who are neurodivergent also bring important skills, insights, and gifts to the context of ministry. Rev. Kay says,

> We tend to be resilient in the face of surprises or emergencies, mostly because we experience more of them because we forget things. We make connections other people don't, sometimes in ways that are surprisingly insightful and honestly, I've surprised myself that way several times. And having a slightly different perspective on the world often allows us to see problems coming that other folks won't.

Giving an illustration of the abilities for neurodivergent folks to have a different perspective than neurotypical folks, Rev. Kay says,

We're looking at different sides of the same building: neurotypical people see one side, and it's perhaps the most used side or the most familiar side to most folks. Folks with conditions like ADHD see the building from a slightly different angle, and we have information they don't, but we also don't have information they do have. But because neurotypical people are so numerous, they tend to share the information they have (at great volume!) and so we can learn most of it ourselves that way, though there are still sometimes holes we miss. Whereas it is apparently super difficult and complicated for them to try to learn the information we have.

Ministering with Multiple Mental Health Diagnoses and Neurodiversity

Rev. Rachel Noël was diagnosed with Autism, ADHD, and bipolar disorder as an adult. She serves in the Church of England and has experienced firsthand the fear, ignorance, prejudice, and stigma still surrounding mental health diagnoses and neurodiversity in society, particularly in the church. She says that in the church there are assumptions made about the abilities of people with neurological disabilities all the time.

Rev. Rachel says one myth in the church is that "Autistic people can't be pastoral or show empathy" and that you can't be a minister if you are neurodivergent. Church law allows bishops to exclude candidates from ordination based on assumptions about their physical or mental health. Rev. Rachel herself has experienced ableism in several forms, including from people who question her fitness to be ordained since she is neurodivergent. Other clergy members tell her she will be saved from disabilities when she goes to heaven; people have prayed for the demons to come out of her. Statements like this cause spiritual harm.

Rev. Rachel said,

I think we still have a long way to go to really value neurodivergent people in our churches and in our communities. We are often expecting people to behave and think a certain way, and those that are different can make us feel uncomfortable. Often we find it easier to exclude those who challenge us, or seek to distract or entertain them, rather than to be curious, to listen, to get to know and understand. It's easier to treat people who are different just as recipients of pastoral care—to want to look after them, to care for them, but still to treat them as "other," to keep them at arm's length.... unless or until they can conform to our expectations of them.

She encourages other neurodivergent ministers to find congregations where they can be open about their neurodiversity and honest about the gifts they bring and the supports they need. For Rev. Rachel, it's additional administrative support that allows her to use her gifts to serve the church.

For me, that includes sharing my creativity and communication; my gift for seeing the big picture, process, strategy, and connections; my curiosity and passion for excellence; and my willingness to keep asking questions. ... I've learned to use my creativity in exploring my faith, to encounter God.

When neurodivergent ministers are supported and encouraged to share their gifts with the church, we experience God's gift of blessed minds. Rev. Rachel asks important questions for the church when she says: "What would it take to value the faith stories of those with brains and bodies that work differently to ours? Are we willing to see Christ working in each other?"[72]

Insights from NeuroWild

Emily "Em" Hammond is a neurodiversity educator and advocate who creates resources she wished she had had for herself and her own family. She says this about the core values embedded in her work: "It is not about having all the answers in the moment, but rather, choosing a path forward that is not going to damage the mental well-being of the student." The NeuroWild approach prioritizes mental health and positive self-image. On her social media bio, she identifies as "Autistic and ADHD Speech Pathologist, illustrator, artist, and Mum to three kiddos." Em shares her work on the social media page "NeuroWild" and lives in New South Wales, Australia. Yet her reach is global. With thousands of followers on social media, the church can learn a lot from her wisdom and her research. She actively shares updates on her social media page with advice, tips, and best practices for neuroinclusivity. Em created "The NeuroWild Shift," which is an easy-to-use approach for supporting neurodivergent students.

As the church strives to honor its neurodivergent minsters, staff, and their families, it is important to hear what Em shares that has been helpful to her. She says it is important to break the silence about neurodiversity and to inform people about brain differences and mental health realities. Breaking the silence is important is because the silence adds to the stigma and shame of being different. About being neurodivergent, Em says: "We feel different. We can tell we're different."[73] She says breaking the silence can help better understand brain differences and help people feel good about being different.

Ministry is often stressful, overwhelming, and tiring. This is true especially for neurodivergent folks in ministry. As a professional, Em breaks the silence about what it is like for her to experience stress as a neurodivergent person. "I can't learn when I'm scared. I can't focus when I'm stressed. I can't do good work when I'm anxious. I can't follow instructions properly when I feel threatened. I can't find the persistence to do hard things when I'm overwhelmed." She says she needs to feel safe in order to feel calm. "And safety does not come from yelling, threatening, or fear. It comes from empathy, connection, and coregulation."[74] For neurodivergent ministers encountering conflict with church leaders, there need to be additional accommodations in place that will support the minster's needs. Perhaps accommodation looks like permission to take a break from a conversation, leave the room, or take additional time to process thoughts, feelings, and emotions.

Neurodivergent professionals can face discrimination in the workplace, including the church. Em talks about common issues that neurodivergent professionals face in the workplace when it comes to communication style. She says when it comes to neurodivergent folks, there can be complaints of "tangential communication, difficulty staying on topic, erratic communication, [events or conversations being] disjointed, and poorly planned." The power of breaking the silence is the opportunity to address these realities and work together to put in place accommodations. But there needs to be safety in doing so, and not fear of being fired or punished for advocating for support.

Em says these complaints about communication styles of neuro-divergent folks are examples of ableism and a preference for neurotypical communication styles.

> Linear communication is but one way of doing it. It's all well and good. But it's not the way I do it. Many neurodivergent people do it differently. We jump between topics. We link ideas

in a non-linear way. We connect ideas so quickly in our minds that we don't necessarily explain every step of the thought process. We might forget bits and then circle back. And that's ok.

What would it look like for congregations to create supportive and accommodating work environments for neurodivergent ministers based on nonlinear communication styles?

Em advocates for neurodivergent ways of being a professional to be honored and celebrated in the world.

> We're allowed. Our way is expressive. It's creative. It's a lot of fun. And it tends to be appreciated by other neurodivergent folk. So. If you are uncomfortable with the way we communicate, perhaps you might write yourself a goal to develop your understanding and acceptance of neurodivergent communication styles. Yes?[75]

As a professional who is part of a neurofamily, Em offers the church an example of the beauty of knowledge and celebrating the power of neurodiversity. Faith communities can celebrate the leadership of neurodivergent ministers and honor their gifts. Churches can also be safe and supportive communities for ministers to discover their own neurodiversity, perhaps even later in life. For example, Em was a thirty-five-year-old parent of three when she found out she was Autistic. "Knowing that about myself helped me to understand so much. About myself, my kids, my friends, my family. I love knowing. I love analyzing it all. I love finding connections. I especially love finding other neurokin who get me. I guess all I mean is, I'm so glad to be here."[76] Em helps the church imagine a world where neurokin belong in beloved community.

Imagine a neuroinclusive church, led by neurodivergent ministers, creating beloved community where everyone is celebrated and loved. What would it look like to "NeuroWild" the church, celebrating the beauty in diversity and honoring the presence of the divine in all brains, all bodies, and all humans?

Ministering with a Neurodivergent Family

It's one thing for a minister to be neurodivergent; it's a whole other thing to be part of a neurofamily in ministry. Neurofamilies sometimes have caregivers and child(ren) who identify as neurodivergent. Congregations are not only the places where ministers work; they are also the environment that shapes the minister's family. When ableism affects a neurodivergent pastor, it also affects their family. Tragically, harmful words and actions occur when congregational members, lay leaders, and staff are not educated about neurodiversity. Ministers and their families can experience discrimination, ableism, and trauma as a result of discrimination from the church toward their neurofamily.

Rev. Nina Merkle Nestlerode is an ordained minister in the Christian Church (Disciples of Christ) and is mother to a neurodivergent teen. She identifies as part of a neurofamily and courageously shares her story of church hurt, with the blessing of her son and her husband, and they hope their family's story will serve as a cautionary tale for congregations. Stories like Rev. Nina's are all too common yet not openly talked about because of the shame and stigma in churches. As you read Rev. Nina's story, imagine how you would have responded if you were involved. Imagine what the congregation could have done to prevent the harm. Imagine what God is calling you to do to support families like Rev. Nina's.

∞ Story Illustration (As Told by Rev. Nina)

Just as our son was ending third grade, our family accepted a new call in a different state where my clergy spouse and I served as co-senior pastors. The congregation was friendly, warm, vibrant and well known in the community as solid and generous. They welcomed all kinds of people at their community meal, served four nights a week in conjunction with partnering congregations. Yet our son struggled and acted out in, of all places, the elementary school Sunday School room. Our son had IEP accommodations at his previous school that worked wonders for his focus and reducing his anxiety and overstimulation. One of these was having something to fidget with in his hands.

Yet the Sunday School class was long taught by three retired (and well respected) teachers, now in their seventies and approaching their eighties. Unbeknownst to us as parents, they refused to let him hold anything in his hands. As he nervously shuffled around, they would tell him more sternly to sit still and quietly in his chair. He had come from a church with interactive lessons, movement and "wondering" questions to speak out to with enthusiasm. This was so different for him. He reacted strongly and told them he needed his fidget item. The teachers (there were always two in the room, sometimes three) began to grab his fidget item from his hands and place it on a high shelf. He acted out, and as this continued, the problem grew more extreme.

I worked with the teachers, explained his needs, sat in on classes to model more open and soothing inclusion. Yet, any time I was not there, they were more stern with him and again took away his fidget item, at times grabbing it and prying it from his hand. My spouse and I were perplexed and concerned. As pastors, where could we find safety and inclusion for our child? The pressure to have him attend was everyone's expectation, but it left us wondering if we could pull him out.

We eventually learned that one of the teachers had her own health issues and grew frustrated with him when he wasn't following her strict methods. She would be harsh with him at times. Our son felt trapped, resentful, and heartbroken as he missed his previous church community and wondered if church could ever love him or be a safe place for him again. One of the other teachers talked with me and explained the health concerns and behaviors. Yet because they had been friends for decades, she was unwilling to step in to guide as she worried she would hurt her friend's feelings. Instead, she wanted our young son to be the one to practice compassion and understanding for the teacher rather than the other way around. The third teacher, despite my calm repeated explanations of his neurodiverse diagnosis and needs, chose to disregard the information we provided about our son and instead sent me emails about specific brain disorders, assuming a rare condition that her young extended family member had must be what was troubling my son. Our efforts to provide information, training and guidance for ways to create a welcoming, inclusive learning environment for our son were unsuccessful, even when we brought this to the Christian Education Chair and other Board and Pastoral Relations Committee members.

We served that congregation for less than two years. As we became more determined to care for our son's needs, we were dismissed, gossiped about, and rejected. Our son had been baptized at this congregation. The pain of his being outcasted, diminished and bullied by the teachers deeply hurt him emotionally.

For a few years, he inquired about being rebaptized in a community that loved him and understood him. Unfortunately, the pandemic years paused this. Our son is now a vibrant teenager flourishing in life (high school, our new church, clubs, and other activities, church youth group, Sunday School, etc.)—all because of teachers and leaders that are willing to adapt, learn and lead with compassion and love first. He knows he belongs and is loved, as well as he is an equally loving part of the community. His gifts are seen and encouraged. Praise be to God!

Reflection Question

What can we learn from Rev. Nina's story about the risks neurodivergent children and their families face in congregations that are not educated about neurodiversity and therefore do not support neurofamilies?

CHAPTER TEN

The Neurospiritual Movement

Neurodivergent
It's my life. It's my journey.
To my wonder brain

Neurodiversity Parable of the Blessed Minds

Before Jesus ascended into heaven, he took one last long walk along the road with his beloved disciple. They walked side by side, passing by olive trees where birds of the air made their nest.

She asked Jesus, "Is being neurodivergent a way of life?"

And Jesus said, "It's more than a way of life: it's how we are made in God's image."

And she said, "But I feel lonely, like I am the only one who is different."

And Jesus said, "Wherever you go, my Spirit will go with you on this journey. My beloved, your brain is filled with wonder, and your mind is blessed."

Key Words in Chapter Ten

Blessed minds: The affirmation and celebration that neurodivergent people are blessed by God.

Lived experience: Firsthand account, knowledge, insight, and wisdom because it is part of a person's life.

Neurospirituality: What happens when a neurodivergent person of faith experiences an encounter with the holy.

***

Blessed Minds

Blessed are the crazy. Blessed are the marriages and civil unions. Blessed are the youth. Blessed are the minds. My journey is one of blessings, and I proclaim the power of blessing not only in my life but also in yours. I invite you to join me in experiencing the blessings available to each one of us in this life. No matter who you are or where you are on your mental health journey, there is a blessing waiting just for you. It's not up to me to describe it for you or to define it for you, only to invite you to be open to discovering the divine blessings all around you and within you.

I know firsthand the intensity of emotional and mental health experiences that leave you depleted, desperate, and ready to give everything up. I know the feeling of being so overwhelmed that you just want to slip out of your body and disappear. I also know the feeling of a love so much bigger than I can comprehend. I know the compassionate embrace of a Spirit that holds me close.

In a world overflowing with reasons to curse God and die, it is an act of courageous hope to be open to being blessed. I believe with all my heart, mind, body, and soul that we are designed to be vessels of blessings. I believe we are whole, holy, and blessed. There's no diagnosis, illness, disability, disease, or experience that can ever take away your divine blessing.

That's why I wrote this book, *Blessed Minds*. I wanted to share with you my dreams about the ways we can create communities that invite all of us to show up, just as we are, without judgment, shame, stigma, or fear. Mental health experiences and neurodiversity expressions are still faced with stigma. The world can change. We can be better to one another and to ourselves.

I also wrote this book to explore my personal experiences with mental health and mental health diagnoses. As I navigate the world in recovery and treatment for complex post-traumatic stress disorder, I have intermittent episodes of depression and anxiety that are triggered by stressful events. Most of the time I can use my coping skills, work with my therapist, and manage to get through the day feeling good. But sometimes, even with all my mental health tools, it is hard to take the next deep breath.

I have personally experienced ableism and discrimination in the institutional church. One example was in a one-on-one work meeting in a colleague's office. After we had discussed a disagreement about a strategic approach, he stood up from the table at which we were both sitting and yelled, "You are crazy!" Because I did not agree with him, he got angry. I believe he was trying to intimidate me and he was frustrated by my different way of seeing things, my neurodivergence. I experienced his words and actions as degrading and dehumanizing.

When I reported this episode to my supervisor, the response was for this abusive colleague to invite me out to lunch. No, thank you. This experience traumatized me and made the work environment emotionally unsafe. Thankfully, with support from my therapist, family, and friends, I was able to transition into a new ministry setting. Looking back at this experience through the lens of my own neurodiversity, I have more compassion for myself and regret that I did not know how to better advocate for myself. I am humbled by my own blessed mind and my utter dependence on other people to keep me grounded, to keep me held in love and prayer.

In the spring of 2023, a year after engaging with Dr. Kimberly Douglass' work about race and neurodiversity, I found myself talking with Dr. Michael Cartledge, who teaches at Princeton Theological Seminary. I was a guest lecturer for his course "Neurodiversity Class on Mental Health and Young People," and he told me that more and more of his students are self-identifying as neurodivergent. Many of these students will graduate from seminary seeking work in the church and outside of the church. How will the church welcome all of their neurodivergent gifts? What does it mean that God continues to call neurodivergent people into ministry? If we are all made in the image of God, then is God neurodivergent?

What does it mean to think about God as neurodivergent? What does it mean for the church to "do justice, and to love kindness, and to walk humbly with your God" (Micah 6:8), when we engage in ministry by, with, and for neurodiverse communities?

How might embracing a theology of neurodiversity contribute to mental health and disability justice? Does self-identifying as neurodivergent help decrease stigma and shame traditionally associated with mental illness, mental health challenges, brain disorders, and disabilities?

What power does this shift in understanding and interpretation of our identities have in the ongoing transformation and redemption of creation? How might creative theologies of a Neurodivergent God contribute to the salvation story of humankind? Since shame and stigma are significant barriers to accessing mental health resources, support, and accommodations, theologies celebrating neurodiversity can help shift conversations and create pathways for saving lives, decreasing suicide among neurodivergent folks.

What did Dr. Cartledge mean when he said that his seminary students are self-identifying as neurodivergent? In my work with church lay leaders and ministers serving on committees that oversee the process to ordain people to ministry, I am frequently called upon to provide education for the committee about disabilities and mental health. Usually this comes in the aftermath of a committee struggling with ableism toward the candidate for ordained ministry. I sense that most people on these committees would also not know what to do with a candidate openly talking about being neurodivergent. Too often, committees view disability and neurodivergence as barriers to ordination. In my research for this book, neurodivergent seminary students have shared with me about their experience time and time again of ableism.

A neurodivergent young adult who is completing seminary training and working with a committee to be ordained told me, "The ordination process—let alone obtaining and maintaining employment—is incredibly ableist towards those with brain differences and disabilities alike. ... I've witnessed firsthand how isolating that feels when you also have to balance your ND (neurodivergence) with your call." She emphasized that journeying through the path of ordination can be filled with hardships because of ableism in the church when neurodivergent folks are expected to mask. She said it's important for the church to provide support and accommodations so they don't feel "alone in this troubling time (and it *is* a lonely place to be most of the time)."

I hope this book can be a helpful resource as the church supports its neurodivergent ministers, as well as those training and preparing for ordination. What supports and accommodations can the church provide for seminary students, student ministers, and those in the process of ordination? How can we ensure that candidates for ministry will not be discriminated against for being neurodivergent? What will it take for the church to realize neurodivergent people are some of the most gifted peopled God could call to go into ministry?

The language of mental health and disabilities continues to evolve, shaped by medical, social, and cultural models. My own journey of understanding faith and mental health includes exploration of language that reflected my cultural context growing up in a White, Midwestern Christian family in the 1980s. Because there were silence, shame, and stigma associated with serious mental illness, I had no role modeling in how to talk about mental health challenges.

When we did talk in my family about the stressors of serious mental illness of both my father and brother, we used the word "crazy" to describe ourselves. Even while this word carries significant baggage, it is what we chose as the best description of the chaos, unpredictability, instability, struggle, confusion, and discomfort of our experiences.

Evolution of My Blessed Mind

After I wrote about my experiences in my first book, *Blessed Are the Crazy*, there was understandably some pushback for my choice of language in describing my personal experiences in my family of origin. This healthy interrogation of language is appropriate and needs to continue as our understanding of neurobiology brings insight to our human experiences of neurodiversity.

Just as not everyone's favorite color is pink, not everyone will identify with the word "crazy." Some will be offended by it, just as they would be offended by someone driving a pink car. Some will love it. A hot pink car sounds amazing! A key consideration is the ethical commitment to "do no harm." If language is harmful to self or others, we can honor ourselves and others by being open to adapting our language.

For example, I only use the word "crazy" to self-identify. I do not use it to describe others. Actually, I am using the word "crazy" less and less. As a lifelong learner, I am evolving in my thinking, growing, changing, and deepening my understanding of the intersections of mental health, disability, justice, and faith.

Twenty years after graduating from high school, meeting over coffee at the Broadway Diner in my hometown, I asked my high school boyfriend what he remembered about me. He said, "You were cute, sweet, and a nerd." Does being a nerd make me neurodiverse? For me, my identity is more than the labels others put onto me. Being a lifelong nerd who also is in active recovery from complex post-traumatic stress disorder feels like a neurodivergent identity. I find myself now in mid-life still figuring out my unfolding identities as a child of God. Perhaps this is the organic, ever-evolving nature of the brainforest? Like the forest, we constantly change, grow, and experience seasons of loss, death, and rebirth. Like the forest, we do not stand alone but are surrounded by kindred spirits. Like the forest, we are connected by a sometimes invisible bond that roots us in the power of God's love.

The word "neurodivergent" feels like a better fit these days. As I try it on for myself, it feels good, like a new jacket that seems tailor-made for an atypical body type. The sleeves come right to the wrist, the interior lining is silky smooth, and when buttoned up I feel ready to go on stage with the best that I've got. I am still getting used to thinking of myself as neurodivergent, and I am a bit cautious about putting myself in a box. But is that my neurodivergence showing?

In my work with disability and mental health justice communities, I've learned about other words being used. The word "mad" is becoming more common as a way to refer to people with mental health disabilities. My friend Allison self-identifies as "mad and crip" to express her experiences living in a disabled mind and body. For me the word "mad" triggers my complex post-traumatic stress disorder from growing up in a family with episodes of explosive anger and "madness." To me "mad" sounds violent and feels oppressive, weighing heavily on my chest as I consider it for myself. It literally gets harder for me to breathe when I think about the word "mad." Language matters. Language is personal and political. Language can empower us, and it can diminish us. Language can revive us, and it can extinguish the spark of light within us.

As I learn more about the neurodiversity movement, I listen closely to disabled activists, artists, and community members who identify as Black, Indigenous, and People of Color (BIPOC) and I am grateful for their deep wisdom. I am inspired by voices such as Leah Lakshmi Piepzna-Samarasinha and her reflections about the power and joy of self-identifying as part of the neurodiversity movement. She writes in her book *The Future is Disabled: Prophecies, Love Notes, and Mourning Songs*: "Then there's joyful parts of why the world is becoming more and more disabled. Fueled by the bold work of neurodivergent people, especially BIPOC neurodivergent people, more and more people are joyfully coming out as neurodivergent and/or Autistic every day."[77]

The language of neurodiversity opens up space in my chest to breathe deeply, filling my body with positive energy. It's a shift for me, and it feels like an invitation to explore. Thank you for exploring this new-to-me landscape alongside me. I wondered throughout the time researching and writing this book if understanding mental health experiences and symptoms through the lens of neurodiversity might help reduce the stigma and shame still associated with mental health realities. I dream of a day when there is no more stigma and shame.

I wondered if the positive self-identity of neurodivergent would have helped save my sixteen-year-old niece's life from suicide. If she could have understood her own mind as blessed instead of broken, would she still be alive today? If she could have made positive connections to others in the neurodiversity community, would she have found a place to belong?

Yet, as I conclude writing this book, I am struck once again by the burden of labels, how limiting and incomplete they feel, even good ones like neurodivergent. Personally, I don't love being labeled anything, and I don't want to be limited by a label. I just want to be myself—my ever evolving, transforming self. I don't want to be called depressed, crazy, anxious, hysterical, possessed, sad, traumatized, or quiet. I prefer to use terms like neurodiversity and neurodivergent as categories of understanding so I can be more compassionate toward myself and others. If I have learned anything, it's that we still have a lot to figure out when it comes to breaking the silence, creating supportive communities, advocating for justice, and meeting our emotional, mental, physical, and spiritual needs.

It is progress to embrace neurodiversity as a way to honor and celebrate the gifts that come with the vast array of blessed minds. The medical, social, and cultural models of mental health and disability typically gloss over the complexity and nuances of the uniqueness of the individual. The term "neurodiversity" makes it known that each blessed mind is to be celebrated.

We've come a long way from "crazy" (though I do continue to reclaim this word for myself, when I feel like it, as a way to heal the harm done to me). And I am grateful. I wonder where we are headed next. Where do you sense the Spirit leading you? Leading your faith community? Leading us? What conversations need to happen for you to follow where you are being called to lead? How might you and your story be part of God's story in the unfolding neurodiversity movement? How do you see yourself helping to break the silence about neurodiversity and helping to end the stigma and shame?

We are living in an exciting time that calls for experimentation in ministry and theology. I pray that there will continue to be new generations of people answering God's call to use all the gifts God has given us for God's glory. Where do we go from here?

What's next for the neurodiversity and spirituality movement? As we continue in conversation, how should our understanding and language evolve? Worlds create worlds together. Let's create worlds in which we can be ourselves and survive, worlds in which we want to live, worlds in which we can be free.

The Neurospirituality Movement

Blending together neurodiversity and spirituality honors the Spirit that enlivens our blessed minds. As I wondered about where I fit into the neurodiversity movement and where others who are people of faith belong, I felt God nudging me to expand the boundaries of the conversation. I began to daydream about new words to describe what I was sensing within my own mind, body, and spirit. I wondered what word could be coined to describe this experience of being a neurodivergent person who is also spiritual. Using the base word "neuro"—which means nervous system, consisting of the brain and spine—how does this blend with other concepts related to faith and spirituality and the people engaged in this work? Imagine a world connected through a new neurospirituality movement. Like the roots of trees connected in an underground network, as part of the neurodiversity brainforest, we, too, are connected in a neurospiritual movement of the Spirit.

Here are the words born from the union of neurodiversity and faith experiences that began to flow from the stream of my imagination:

Neurosaint

Neuro-Christ

Neurodisciple

Neurospirit

Neurounique

Neurochurch

Neurominister

Neurotheology

Neuroflock

Neuroshepherd

Neurochristology

Neuroecclesiology

And finally, neurospirituality.

Playing with Neurospirituality

Dr. Lisa Miller's book *The Awakened Brain: The New Science of Spirituality and Our Quest for an Inspired Life*[78] highlights what science shows about the brain as the hub for our spirituality. Miller says that our brains have a spiritual docking station inside of them. In short, we are wired to be spiritual. We have the science to prove what mystics have experienced all along: that there is a connection between our neurodiversity and our spirituality, and it is a physical reality located in our brains.

As I reflect on my own mental health and spiritual journey, I've often wondered over the years if what I experienced was a manifestation of mental illness or of God. As a person who experiences mystical visions and sensory manifestations of God's presence, I continually question and doubt their source. I ask myself and my therapist, "Is this of God? Or am I crazy?" Expanding the neurodiversity conversation to include spirituality creates space for people like me. When I consider my spiritual realities, which often seem atypical, they make sense in the framework of neurodiversity.

Neurospirituality is what happens when a neurodivergent person of faith experiences an encounter with the holy. My faith journey is one of ongoing encounters with the holy. One way I carve out time and space for the holy as a busy pastor is through a monthly day of prayer. With the congregation's blessing, I spend one day a month at an affordable local retreat center where there is a covered front porch with a swing, a garden with a bench among the wildflowers, and a quiet room with a little desk overlooking a large oak tree. My neurodivergent brain luxuriates in the silence, in walking in the garden, in sitting in the sunshine, in the array of healthy foods and snacks arranged thoughtfully on the counter, including dark chocolate and strong coffee.

Neurospirituality is a way to understand the different ways in which neurodivergent people nurture their relationship to God. My spirituality deepens in spaces of mental safety, where I can relax my mind, soothe my senses, and recover from the often overstimulating and overwhelming aspects of life and ministry. There is a lot of holy noise in ministry. It's easy to become overwhelmed in ministry by all the demands. As a neurodivergent minister, I need to regularly take time to process, sort through, let go of, and pray about everything that is happening.

My monthly days of prayer are a gift to my blessed mind and a gift to my partners in ministry. Taking a day of prayer gives me a time in which

I connect to God, to myself, and to all the people for whom God invites me to pray and for whom God wants me to care. During my day of prayer, I pray through movement, spending time alone walking in gardens and in the woods. Through movement of my body, I connect to God's Spirit. Neurospirituality invites me—and you—into spiritual accommodations that enable us to flourish in our faith, such as opportunities to nurture our spirit in ways that are meaningful to us.

Neurospirituality is also about encounters with the holy that may seem atypical or surprising. One encounter with the holy I am still processing to this day unfolded in the late summer of 2022. The day after my testimony at a rally in the atrium of the Indiana State House supporting reproductive rights, severe pain related to my reproductive organs led me to the emergency room. I experienced a rare and extremely painful ovarian torsion. This quickly led me down the path to a radical hysterectomy at the age of forty-five. During my medical leave and recovery, I sought out spiritual tools and support to help assist my healing journey.

One of my spiritual directors encouraged me to create a "Montessori" environment by my bed—various activities for me to engage in to help me relax and pass the time. On my nightstand I made an altar out of mandala coloring books, colored markers, prayer books, a candle, an icon of Mary, an icon of Mary Magdalene, a wooden figurine from the Holy Land of Mary holding baby Jesus, and a big cup of water. Guided by my intuition, spiritual mentors, doctors, nurses, family, and friends, I allowed my bodymind to rest deeply and fully in the tender love of the Spirit.

Inspired by the book *Birthing the Holy: Wisdom from Mary to Nurture Creativity and Renewal*[9] by Christine Valters Painter, I began experimenting with the prayer tool of the rosary. This was all new to me, but I felt led by the Spirit to expand my spiritual practices. After all, millions of people use the rosary to pray. Why not me? In her book, Painter encourages readers unfamiliar with the rosary to go on Etsy and choose a rosary that "speaks" to them. On my first day home from the hospital, I ordered a handmade rosary made of rose quartz crystals. The rosary artist described the process of creating her rosaries as a way to find comfort and peace in the aftermath of the death of both her parents within a short period of time. I was drawn to the artist's story and her beautiful design.

The day the rosary arrived in the mail I was still spending most of the day lying in bed and resting during my early recovery. Holding the rosary in my hands, I lay down in bed to rest. As I prayed, I lifted up the name of Mary Magdalene, beloved of Jesus. I asked for her loving presence to fill me with their healing light and love. I felt led to lay the rosary across my midsection, positioning the rose quartz crystals and the figurine of Mary on the part of my body's flesh above what was once my womb. The rosary made a large oval shape across my body. A waterfall of peace rushed over me.

As the rosary laid draped over my body, I felt embraced by the divine, tenderly loved and cared for. I grieved at the thought of no longer carrying my womb. Yet, during this healing encounter with the rosary and the divine love of Mary Magdalene, I realized my truest womb now resided within my heart. God gave me this beautiful vision of the womb of my heart still able to give birth to joy and love.

I'm tempted to question this mystical encounter as just one of my "crazy" mind tricks. Yet, now I know this tendency to doubt myself is rooted in self-stigma and shame. My encounters with God through visions are real. Just like a rainbow in the sky is real. As I reflect on my spiritual journey, I wonder about Mary Magdalene and her own blessed mind. Perhaps Mary Magdalene was neurodivergent. After all, she never really fit into the crowd of other disciples. She was almost always misunderstood. Her brain worked differently from the others, and so did her heart. Yes, Mary Magdalene's mind was divinely blessed.

Self-identifying as neurodivergent places me in a lineage of neurodivergent siblings in the faith. There are saints who have gone before us and more generations to come of people whose minds are blessed by God's gift of neurodiversity. Praise be for our neurodivergent ancestors! Embracing the fact that my brain works differently is a form of self-love that is healing and holy.

My encounter of spiritual healing during my experience of disability is what I am calling neurospirituality: my neurodivergent self, experiencing profound spiritual realities because of my brain differences. I believe it is because of the brain differences God gave me that I am able to experience God this way. This permission to encounter the holy, right where we are at and just as we are, is the heart of the neurospirituality of blessed minds. My blessed mind is neurospiritual.

The freedom to play is also at the heart of neurospirituality. Rev. Katie Hays of Galileo Church believes there is a connection between a childlike playful spirit and neurodiversity. I experience this within myself. When I am most free to be who I am as neurodivergent, I feel a deep childlike joy bubble up within me. The spirit of playfulness roots me in the Spirit's joy. Research at the intersection of spirituality and neurodiversity is an emerging field, but some important findings are starting to surface.

Erin Raffety, co-creator of the Brainforest online course at Princeton Theological Seminary and author of the book *From Inclusion to Justice: Disability Ministry and Congregational Leadership*, researched how faith formation and spirituality for neurodivergent folks could be experienced through gaming, specifically using Minecraft.[80] What she discovered is that "play and spirituality are not separate endeavors but contiguous practices that the church has overlooked when it comes to spiritual formation." Play is too often viewed as "unproductive," and Raffety says this view is rooted in ableism. She says the church "prioritizes biblical learning and knowledge over fun and fellowship," and this perpetuates ableism.

Including playful fellowship experiences as important parts of the life of the church makes a church more neuroinclusive. Raffety's research shows that "play for play's sake in Christian community is a worthwhile endeavor." Churches can include neurodivergent folks to help them make spirituality and faith formation more accessible and equitable, but they need to be invited into these leadership roles. By honoring playfulness as spiritual, neuroinclusive ministry creates opportunities for play as integral to faith formation.

For neurospirituality and for neurodivergent folk to flourish as leaders, we do well to embrace the importance of play and fellowship. Neurospirituality embraces play as a spiritual discipline. The biggest barrier to making church accessible to neurodivergent folks are the neurotypical concepts and structures of Christian education. Raffety concludes that Christian cultures in the U.S. glorify productivity and that churches view play as superfluous. Neurospirituality reclaims play as a sacred act. Our minds are blessed when we are free to play. Raffety concludes her research on this topic of neurodiversity and spirituality by saying that spaces to play "are vital points of accessibility, collaboration, and spiritual connection for neurodiverse groups that are in short supply within churches"[81] It's time for us, the church, to bless the playfulness of the neurodivergent Body of Christ.

As we play and experiment with the intersections of faith, spirituality, and neurodiversity, I pray that we create spaces to share ourselves authentically with one another. I pray that we make spaces to play. I pray that we feel free to share our stories of neurodiversity and faith. I pray that the voices of neurodivergent folks among us not be silenced by stigma and shame. I pray the church will be welcoming of neurospiritual stories, for there are so many more stories waiting to be told. I pray for neurospiritual folks like me to be engaged and supported in ministry.

Vincent Van Gogh as Patron Saint of Neurodivergent Ministers

At church in my pastor's office across from my desk on the wall is a replica of Vincent Van Gogh's almond tree painting titled *Almond Blossom*. He painted it while in a residential program to receive treatment for his mental health. This painting was created to be a gift to celebrate the birth of his brother Theo's first child. Vincent was close to Theo, who often took care of him during his times of need. I marvel at Van Gogh's talent and the depth of beauty and emotions in his artwork. Van Gogh wrote to Theo about the way his own blessed mind worked, saying, "I feel a power within me … a fire that I may not quench, but must keep ablaze."[82]

Van Gogh was neurodivergent and did not get the accommodations he needed as a young man entering ministry. The church kicked him out of ministry because of his "bad" behavior, not following the strict rules of the professional clergy or meeting the church's expectations of him as a minister. His dismissal letter from the Evangelical Committee said they terminated his ministry because "a talent for speaking is indispensable to anyone placed at the head of a congregation. The absence of that quality renders the exercise of an evangelist's principal function wholly impossible. He does not yield to the wishes of the Committee." Van Gogh's biographer writes:[83]

> The constant warnings and rebukes from his superiors, and his own increasingly eccentric behavior, had turned his congregation against him. In meetings, they insulted him and openly mocked his strange ways. The children in his beloved catechism class rebelled against him. No doubt echoing their parents, they called him "*fou*"—crazy—the first time that the word appears in the record.

I feel a deep sadness thinking about Van Gogh's vocational calling to go into ministry being unfulfilled because he never received the support. In the aftermath of the church's rejection, Van Gogh suffered ongoing spiritual, physical, and mental anguish. He loved God and wanted to share that love with the world. After his expulsion from the ministry, Van Gogh was seen wandering the streets in the winter barefoot and in rags, and people would call him "mad." He would answer, "The Lord Jesus was also crazy."[84]

The church did not know what to do with Van Gogh's neurodivergence, so they got rid of him. The church viewed his brain differences as deficits. I believe Van Gogh never recovered from this profound rejection, ableism, and spiritual abuse by the church. Whether intended or not, the church dishonored Van Gogh, and the trauma caused by the church's abuse contributed to Van Gogh's death by suicide.

I dream of a world where Vincent Van Gogh is celebrated by the church for his blessed mind. I dream of a church that provides support and accommodations for the Van Goghs of today who God calls into ministry. Neurodiversity is not a problem for the church to make disappear. Neurodiversity is God showing up, in human form, inviting us into deeper ways of loving one another.

May we, the church, not get in our own way. May the neurodiversity of God's people be our guide, showing us new and creative ways to play together, to dream together, to love one another and share this redeeming love with the world. May all blessed minds be loved.

∞ Story Illustration

Driving my child to school one fall morning, we were talking about the science of rainbows in nature. I said, "It takes both rain and sunlight to make a rainbow. Both shadows and light at the same time."

My child looked at me, waiting for me to make my point.

"That's why I like the infinity rainbow symbol for neurodiversity. It's the gray matter of the brain with the spark of God's light. The raincloud's shadow and the sun's light coming together. That's what makes the rainbow."

My child said, "OK, Mom."

I got more excited and began to feel my own brain light up in rainbow colors.

? Reflection Question

Who else would benefit from reading and discussing *Blessed Minds: Breaking the Silence About Neurodiversity*? How is God calling you to join the neurodiversity spiritual movement?

Benediction

 Things to Remember

You are amazing.

You are beautiful.

You are complex (in a good way!).

You are a beloved human being.

Your brain is different and good.

The fact that you exist is a miracle and a dream come true.

You are here for a reason.

You may not know your reason yet; but trust me, it is a really good one.

Your life is important.

Getting better takes time.

Be patient and gentle with yourself.

You are more than your disability, neurodiversity, diagnosis, or mental health experiences.

It's OK to be different.

It's OK not to be OK for a while (even if it's hard).

Your life matters to God.

Try your best.

Breathe.

Stay.

(Adapted from *Blessed Youth Survival Guide*.)

AFTERWORD

In *Blessed Minds*, Sarah Griffith Lund cites how the mother of disability theology, Nancy Eisland, sought to center the insights and voices of disabled people in her 1994 book *The Disabled God*. But Eiesland was also clear that her book was limited to a focus on physically disabled people—not because she didn't believe in the liberation of all disabled people, but because she felt particularly well-positioned to speak from her experience and that of others to their particular contributions to theology.

Recalling Eiesland's starting point puts in distinct perspective some of the vital theological contributions of *Blessed Minds*. Not only does Lund consider what voices might be masked or silent in disability communities today, but she foregrounds her own experience to cultivate a theology that is both practically and theologically expansive. It's practically expansive because it calls in people whose minds and spirits have been dismissed as abnormal and boldly claims space for neurodivergent people to name both their struggles and their insights. And it's theologically expansive because it subtly calls out the way in which rights-based movements or accommodations have not been and will not be enough when it comes to the Kingdom of God: it charges churches to not just perform but enact justice by radically celebrating diversity.

What's striking is that Eiesland anticipated our collective discomfort with the image of a *Disabled God*, much as I'm sure Lund knows she may receive pushback for her interpretive parables, her Ten Commandments, her invocation of Vincent Van Gogh as the patron saint of neurodiversity, or perhaps most especially, the characterization of God as neurodivergent. As Eiesland wrote,

> [Some have objected that] a model of God that incorporates disability signals confusion for the church, and they insist that a halt shall be called on all representational language for God. With the emergence of African American, feminist, gay-lesbian, and Latin American liberation theologies in recent history, models of God have proliferated. Yet this representational proliferation does not portend chaos; rather it is the corporate enactment of the resurrection of God.*

In a similar way, Lund's book queries where our models of God have not only been too white, too heteronormative, and too American, but

---

* Eiesland, 104-5.

too neuronormative. Perhaps some will try to claim that the language of neurodiversity also "portends chaos" in its broadness and profound diversity. Similar to Eiesland, I think Lund's wisdom here is to draw not only on her own account but precisely on that of scripture as well as other neurodivergent pastors and activists, and even historical figures, from Van Gogh to Gorman, to demand transformation not of neurodivergent people but from a society who diminishes them. Finally, in highlighting the intersectional nature of disability experiences, Lund actually challenges all these representations as precisely too diminished and too fragmented, when it comes to who God actually is and how God sees us.

In the midst of times where society is actively "othering" those who are different, this book could not be more important in its theological convictions, but also its practical insights. We will need prophets like Lund to not only expand our visions for the Kingdom of God but to literally, teach us how to pray. We will need churches and their clergy and lay leaders to be staunch defenders and advocates for beholding the belovedness of God's diversity, seeking justice and working for this capacious vision of the Kingdom. And thankfully in Lund, we have such a pastor and a prophet. May this book embolden neurodivergent people and their advocates everywhere, birthed into such a time as this.

Erin Raffety
Princeton, New Jersey

Appendices

GLOSSARY

⚷━━⚲ Key Words

Ableism: A set of beliefs or practices that devalue and discriminate against people with physical, intellectual, or psychiatric disabilities and often rests on the assumption that disabled people need to be "fixed" in one form or another.[85]

Accessibility: The Office for Civil Rights at the U.S. Department of Education defines accessibility as meaning "when a person with a disability is afforded the opportunity to acquire the same information, engage in the same interactions, and enjoy the same services as a person without a disability in an equally integrated and equally effective manner, with substantially equivalent ease of use."[86]

Accommodation: Any product, adjustment, or service that makes a task or situation easier or more comfortable for someone to handle in their daily life.

ADA: The Americans with Disabilities Act passed in 1990 to ensure the equal rights of disabled people.

ADHD: Attention Deficit Hyperactivity Disorder is a neurological disability affecting one's ability to focus and/or can manifest as impulsive behaviors.

Bipolar: A mental health diagnosis characterized by extreme shifts in mood, energy, and activity.

Blessed minds: The affirmation and celebration that neurodivergent people are blessed by God.

Body of Christ: The community of Jesus followers who represent Jesus' hands, feet, heart, and mind in the world.

Creator: God as the source of all created matter, the artist of all that exists past, present, and future.

Decolonizing: The process of challenging and dismantling systems that perpetuate supremacy, power, and privilege.

Discrimination: Being treated unfairly and unequally for a specific reason.

Disability: According to the United Nations Convention on the Rights of Persons with Disabilities, ratified by at least 182 countries around the world, disability "results from the interaction between persons with impairments and attitudinal and environmental barriers that hinders their full and effective participation in society on an equal basis with others."[87]

Diversity: The range of human differences, including but not limited to race, ethnicity, gender, gender identity, sexual orientation, age, social class, physical ability or attributes, mental health realities, neurodevelopmental abilities, religious or ethical values system, national origin, and political beliefs.[88]

Equity: Providing resources appropriate to the environment to obtain equal outcomes. Imbalances within our social systems result in a need to provide equitable processes.

Fidgets: Objects that can be manipulated by the body. Their use is intended to aid in self-regulation and to help people improve their ability to focus and regulate feelings such as boredom, anxiety, and excitement. Fidgets serve a valuable purpose in the lives of people of all ages.

Genesis: The first book of the Hebrew Bible/Christian Old Testament.

God: The One who is Maker of heaven and earth and the focus of monotheistic religion.

Inclusion: Recognizing and valuing the unique skills, talents, and experiences a person brings to the table.

Interconnectedness: The idea that nothing exists separate from anything else, that all of life is connected, and that what impacts one impacts all.

Intersectionality: The existence of interlocking forms of oppression and their impact on people's lives.

Lived experience: Firsthand account, knowledge, insight, and wisdom because it is part of a person's life.

Mental health: The guiding source for all feelings, thoughts, behaviors, and social connections.

Mental health experiences: The unique mental health realities that can arise from within the brain or from external factors such as stigma, stress, and discrimination.

Mental illness: The interruption of feelings, thoughts, behaviors, and social connections.

Neurodivergent: Having a brain that functions differently from the majority of people's.

Neurodiversity: The range of differences in brain function and behavior among all humans.

Neurofamily: A family in which one or more members is/are neurodivergent.

Neuroinclusive: An approach or environment that actively includes and accommodates people with diverse brain functions.

Neuroqueer: A person who sees their neurodivergent and queer identities interacting and working together in a way they wish to claim/self-identify with.

Neurospicy: A state of being that feels different for each person. As one friend explained it in a text to me, "When my brain is having a hard time processing different things and I am having a hard time with executive functioning skills, I feel all over the place or a hot mess." For some, self-identifying as neurospicy can also be a form of playfulness.

Neurospirituality: What happens when a neurodivergent person of faith experiences an encounter with the holy.

Sensory sensitivity: Sensory differences in the way a person experiences the world through their senses of taste, touch, sight, hearing, smell, and balance.

Shame: The feeling of being worthless, not good enough, or unlovable.

Spirit: The power of life that breathes into every living thing.

Stigma: The negative judgment of people due to particular traits or behaviors they have. Such judgment frequently prevents people from seeking mental health supports.

Stimming: Short for "self-stimulation," repetitive movement or sounds that help a person deal with emotions, stress, sensory input, or focus. Examples include tapping a foot, doodling, pacing back and forth, and twirling hair.

Theology: Conversations about God's relationship with humanity and all of creation.

Trinity: The church doctrine that God is one but made of three expressions, God as parent, God as child, and God as Spirit.

The Ten Commandments of Neurodiversity

1. You shall honor diversity.
2. You shall rest as a form of resistance.
3. You shall not hide your light or cover up what makes you shine.
4. You shall have accommodations to support your flourishing.
5. You shall be respected as a whole person and not be defined by labels, diagnosis, or disease.
6. You shall be included in all aspects of society and given equal opportunities for happiness and success.
7. You shall be honored as created in the image of the divine.
8. You shall be celebrated for the different gifts you bring to the world.
9. You shall be valued as an asset and not a burden to society.
10. You shall be free to be you: to explore, grow, create, and change.

Ten Core Values of Neuroinclusive Ministry

1. Each mind is blessed. Neurodiversity is not a problem to be solved, but a blessing.
2. No ministry benefits from making assumptions about people's identities and what people need. The realities, identities, needs, and accommodations of each unique person are honored, respected, and considered.
3. "Nothing about us without us." Neurodivergent people and their loved ones are involved in the planning, formation, and leadership of the ministry.
4. The context for ministry is grounded in creating healthy boundaries around physical spaces, physical touch, sensitivity to sensory stimulation such as sound and light, clear guidelines and scheduling, and options honoring each person's sense of personal well-being, including freedom of movement.
5. Accommodations are provided with grace and joy, offering multiple and ongoing opportunities for accessibility needs to be expressed and met.

6. The highest priority is building relationships of trust, compassion, and mutual care that create a sense of community.

7. Communication is open and clear, incorporating various forms of written, verbal, and visual, and body language, as well as an openness to communicating in ways that best meet the needs of individuals.

8. Flexibility is valued and change is encouraged to allow for adaptations based on feedback and responses to emerging needs.

9. The goal is belonging, not merely inclusion. Inclusion is what makes it possible for people to be there. Belonging means that you want them there, that they are active members, and that they will be missed if they are not there.

10. The guiding spiritual purpose is sharing the radically powerful and hopeful love of God. This purpose shapes every aspect of ministry. There is no judgment, stigma, or shame allowed.

Ten Steps for Developing a Neuroinclusive Ministry in Your Congregation

These steps are not necessarily sequential. One of the steps may happen before or after other steps on the list. Follow the synergy and Spirit of your congregation. The context and culture of your congregation will also reveal which step may follow another.

1. **Make a commitment.** Before you begin, do some soul searching and spiritual reflection. Starting a neuroinclusive ministry may take considerable time. You need to discern if you are ready to take on a long-term project. It will probably involve sharing your own personal stories about why you are passionate about neurodiversity. This is a "nothing about us without us" type of ministry that needs to include neurodivergent folks from the beginning. Find at least one other person who also has a "calling" to neuroinclusive ministry. Building community is key.

2. **Educate yourself.** Learn all you can about neurodiversity. You probably already know a lot from your own experiences, but it's important to gather information to better understand and be compassionate toward others. You don't need to be an expert in neurodiversity, but work for a basic understanding.

3. **Get buy-in** from your faith leader/minister/board of directors/ or the congregation itself. The lines of communication and decision-making process are different in every congregation. You will want to get the support from the church leadership about what you hope to accomplish and why neuroinclusive ministry is important. You may need to take time to educate them and work through their questions so they view neurodiversity as an important part of the church's growth in mission and ministry. Don't give up if you face some roadblocks.

4. **Form a neuroinclusive ministry team.** Get the word out that you are creating a new ministry team about neurodiversity. Set a time and place for the first meeting and announce it during worship, in the newsletters, and other appropriate places. Make personal invitations to people you know who might bring their lived experiences of neurodiversity to the team. Make the invitation open to anyone who is interested in helping figure out where the Spirit is leading. Consider making your first team meeting a "come and see" and meet over a meal or potluck after worship.

5. **Decide with your team what you want to accomplish.** Define what your hopes are for the beginning of the neuroinclusive ministry. Do you want to offer a neurodiversity support group for families? Do you what to offer educational opportunities? Do you want to host book studies and discussion groups? Do you want to create a resource library? Do you want to create a sensory library? Do you want to do education about mental health, disabilities, and neurodiversity? After you have clarified your hopes and goals, begin to develop a strategy and timeline to achieve the goals. It is important to meet regularly to review plans, envision next steps, and share new resources.

6. **Define strategies for keeping the congregation, leadership, and ministers involved.** Share the mission and goals of the neuroinclusive ministry team with your congregation, your leadership, and ministers, and ask for each group's blessings. Ask each group to help the neuroinclusive ministry team to be successful in serving the needs of the congregation and community. You might ask the congregation to show support by attending educational programs. You might ask the ministers to help support you by including neurodiversity in their sermons and when

they pray. You might focus a weekend or a whole worship service on neurodiversity, especially during Neurodiversity Celebration Month in April. You may ask church leadership to support the neuroinclusive ministry by allocating a small budget for your team's use (for speakers, refreshments, fidgets, etc.).

7. **Make an inventory of available resources.** Poll the members of your team, and find out who they know who might be willing to speak at one of your educational and informational programs. Talk to people working in the field of neurodiversity and people who are neurodivergent and their families to see who will help. Consider creating a resource guide for the congregation.

8. **Join with other organizations.** Find out which congregations, nonprofits, organizations, businesses, and schools in your area have a neurodiversity focus, and meet with them to share ideas and explore collaborations. Consider creating an interfaith network for neurodiversity in your community.

9. **Communicate.** Continue to communicate about your neuroinclusive ministry on an ongoing basis. Consider writing articles for your congregation's newsletter on educational topics and sharing resources. Share on the church website and on social media channels. Announce your activities in worship, and even let the wider community know about your congregation's focus on neurodiversity through community publications and online community groups.

10. **Be prepared to nurture your ministry.** Creating a flourishing neuroinclusive ministry takes more than passion: it also takes persistence, community, and support. Don't get discouraged or burned out. Change takes time, and results may not happen immediately. Keep your spirits lifted, and have fun with this ministry. As Erin Raffety, with the Brainforest, says, embrace playfulness as what it means to do the work of the church. Nurture your spirit and this ministry through play, and let your neurodiversity shine.

(Adapted from "Ten Steps for Developing a Mental Health Ministry in Your Congregation" from Joanne Kelly and Alan Johnson's Interfaith Network on Mental Illness.)

Neurodiversity and Youth Ministry:
Cultivating God's Brainforest

In 2022, with support from the Templeton Foundation and a grant through Fuller Theological Seminary, Michael Paul Cartledge, Erin Raffety and the Institute for Youth Ministry of the Princeton Theological Seminary launched Cultivating God's Brainforest, an online learning module for youth workers that centers and celebrates neurodiversity among young people.

The curriculum is organized in five lessons:

- Lesson 1: Exploring God's Brainforest
- Lesson 2: Prayer and Attention
- Lesson 3: Worship and Senses
- Lesson 4: Love and Expression
- Lesson 5: Flourishing in God's Brainforest

Each lesson has prayer and introductory video, scripture for contemplation, a sermonette video, personal journal reflection prompts, activities for young people and congregation, a congregational connection activity, prompts for online sharing, and audio clips from neurodivergent youth reflecting on each theme. The fifth lesson includes testimonies from neurodivergent youth workers, providing an "it gets better" outlook for neurodivergent youth.

Learn more at online.ptsem.edu/catalog/course/18/neurodiversity-and-youth-ministry

PRINCETON
THEOLOGICAL
SEMINARY

Acknowledgements

Thank you to the big world of neurodiversity and all the folks who have done the work before us!

Thank you to the United Church of Christ Disabilities Ministries and the United Church of Christ Mental Health Network for being companions with me on the journey to build a more just world for all.

Thank you to First Congregational United Church of Christ of Indianapolis, Indiana, and the national setting of the United Church of Christ, my employers, who both gifted me with time for sabbatical the summer of 2023. God gifted me with a vision for writing this book during the sabbatical time.

Thank you to Erin Raffety and Michael Paul Cartledge for sparking the idea for this project, for encouraging me, and for your contributions to this book.

Thank you to Susan Herman for your guidance and support of the manuscript.

I am grateful to the kind, thoughtful, insightful, and critical feedback from trusted friends and colleagues who took the time to be in conversation with me about the topics of mental health, disability, neurodiversity, and the church. Thank you to sensitivity readers: Abbie Chronister, Scott Griffith, Abigail Hale, Cristy Jones, Racheal Keefe, Allie Knofczynski, Ian Lasch, Nina Nestlerod, Gracelynn Norgaard, Kisha Parker, Rudolph (Rudy) Reyes II, and Tarrah Vaupel. Their feedback made this a better book.

Thank you to my publishing family at Chalice Press for making my writing dreams come true.

Heartfelt thanks to my therapist, doctors, teachers, mentors, and friends who support me with encouragement, wisdom, support, and prayer.

Thank you to my family who loves me more than my wildest dreams!

Thanks be and all glory to our Neurodivergent God for making all things possible!

Endnotes

Welcome and Announcements

[1] John Marble, Khushboo Chabria, and Ranga Jayaraman, *Neurodiversity for Dummies* (Hoboken, NJ: Wiley, 2024).

Introduction

[2] Shadae B. Mallory, *Rebel Girls Celebrate Neurodiversity: 25 Tales of Creative Thinkers* (Larkspur, CA: Rebel Girls, Inc., 2024).

[3] Sara Luterman and Kate Sosin, "Who Coined the Term 'Neurodiversity?' Not Judy Singer, Some Autistic Academics Say," *The 19th,* April 23, 2024, https://19thnews.org/2024/04/neurodiversity-term-judy-singer-autistic-advocates/.

[4] John Harris, "The Mother of Neurodiversity: How Judy Singer Changed the World," *The Guardian* Interview, July 5, 2023.

[5] "The Evolution of Autism Symbols Explained," NeuroLaunch, October 24, 2024, https://neurolaunch.com/autism-symbol/.

[6] Steve Silberman, *Neurotribes: The Legacy of Autism and the Future of Neurodiversity* (New York: Avery/Penguin, 2015), 450–51.

[7] Jenara Nerenberg, *Divergent Mind: Thriving in a World that Wasn't Designed for You* (San Francisco, CA: Harper One, 2020).

Chapter One

[8] Marble et al., *Neurodiversity for Dummies*, 24.

[9] Monique Botha, Robert Chapman, Morénike Giwa Onaiwu, Steven K Kapp, Abs Stannard Ashley, and Nick Walker, "The neurodiversity concept was developed collectively: An overdue correction on the origins of neurodiversity theory," *Autism* 28, no.6 (2024): 1591-1594, https://journals.sagepub.com/doi/10.1177/13623613241237871.

[10] Sarah Griffith Lund, *Blessed Are the Crazy: Breaking the Silence About Mental Illness, Family, and Church* (St. Louis, MO: Chalice Press, 2014).

[11] Sarah Griffith Lund, *Blessed Union: Breaking the Silence About Mental Illness and Marriage* (St. Louis, MO: Chalice Press, 2020).

[12] Sarah Griffith Lund, *Blessed Youth: Breaking the Silence About Mental Illness with Children and Teens* (St. Louis, MO: Chalice Press, 2022).

[13] Sarah Griffith Lund, *Blessed Youth Survival Guide* (St. Louis, MO: Chalice Press, 2022).

[14] "Mental health," World Health Organization, accessed September 30, 2024, https://www.who.int/news-room/fact-sheets/detail/mental-health-strengthening-our-response.

[15] "Neurodivergent," Cleveland Clinic, https://my.clevelandclinic.org/health/symptoms/23154-neurodivergent.

[16] Dani Rodwell, "Neurospicy Meaning: What It Is and Where It Came From," NeuroSpark, accessed September 30, 2024, https://www.neurosparkhealth.com/blog/neurospicy-meaning-what-it-means-and-where-it-came-from.html,.

[17] "Teaching Kids About Their Amazing Brain Forests," American Institute for Learning and Human Development blog, December 12, 2019.

[18] Steve Silberman, "Neurodiversity Rewires Conventional Thinking About Brains," *WIRED*, April 16, 2013, https://www.wired.com/2013/04/neurodiversity/.

[19] Thomas Armstrong, *Neurodiversity: Discovering the Extraordinary Gifts of Autism, ADHD, Dyslexia, and Other Brain Differences* (Cambridge, MA: Da Capo Press, 2010), 218.

[20] Sandhya Menon, *The Brain Forest* (Melbourne, Australia: Onwards and Upwards Psychology, 2022).

[21] Amanda Diekman, "A Prayer for Seeking Your Neurodivergence," *Medium*, February 27, 2022,, https://medium.com/artfullyautistic/a-prayer-for-seeking-your-neurodivergence-3d7feb045c89

Chapter Two

[22] Leah Smith, "#Ableism," Center for Disability Rights blog, accessed September 30, 2024, https://cdrnys.org/blog/uncategorized/ableism/.

[23] "Diversity and Inclusion Definitions," Ferris State University, accessed September 30, 2024, https://www.ferris.edu/administration/president/DiversityOffice/Definitions.htm.

[24] Tricia Hersey, *Rest is Resistance: A Manifesto* (New York: Little Brown Spark, 2022).

Chapter Three

[25] Karla Suomala, "Commentary on Genesis 1:1—2:4a," September 8, 2013, https://www.workingpreacher.org/commentaries/narrative-lectionary/creation-3/commentary-on-genesis-11-31-21-4-3.

[26] Suomala, "Commentary on Genesis 1:1—2:4a."

Chapter Four

[27] Nancy Eiesland, *The Disabled God: Toward a Liberation Theology of Disability* (Nashville, TN: Abingdon Press, 1994).

Chapter Five

[28] Leah Smith, "#Ableism," Center for Disability Rights blog, accessed September 30, 2024, https://cdrnys.org/blog/uncategorized/ableism/.

[29] Robert Chapman, *Neurodiversity Studies: A New Critical Paradigm*, "Defining Neurodiversity for Research and Practice," Chapter 14 (New York: Routledge, 2020).

[30] "Suicide Data and Statistics," U.S. Centers for Disease Control and Prevention, https://www.cdc.gov/suicide/facts/data.html.

[31] "Risk Factors, Protective Factors, and Warning Signs," American Foundation for Suicide Prevention, https://afsp.org/risk-factors-protective-factors-and-warning-signs/#:~:text=Depression%20is%20the%20most%20common,unaddressed%2C%20increase%20risk%20for%20suicide.

[32] Sunita Theiss, "Becoming a Church for a People of All Abilities," *Christianity Today*, September 20, 2024 https://www.christianitytoday.com/2024/09/church-for-people-with-disabilities-autism/

Chapter Six

[33] "Understanding the Definition of Accessibility," Equity & Access, accessed September 30, 2024, https://www.ace-ed.org/understanding-the-definition-of-accessibility/.

[34] Harold H. Wilke, "'Mainstreaming' The Alienated: The Church Responds to a 'New' Minority," *The Christian Century*, March 23, 1977, Disability History Museum, https://www.disabilitymuseum.org/dhm/lib/detail.html?id=1721&page=2, accessed September 30, 2024.

Chapter Seven

[35] Lauren Rose Strand, "Charting Relations Between Intersectionality Theory and the Neurodiversity Paradigm, *Disability Studies Quarterly,* 2017.

[36] Amy Crawford, "Encounters at the Well: Celebrating Intersectionality," December 13, 2021, https://www.ucc.org/celebrating-intersectionality/.

[37] Crawford, "Encounters."

[38] Crawford, "Encounters."

[39] Kimberly Douglass, "Loving Diverse Minds, Leading Diverse Hearts: The Way to a Human-Centered Future," *Future Hearts and Minds*, accessed September 30, 2024, https://futureheartsandminds.substack.com/.

[40] Douglass, "Loving Diverse Minds."

[41] "Resources to Host Your Mental Health Sunday Year-round," United Church of Christ Mental Health Network, accessed September 30, 2024, https://www.mhn-ucc.org/mental-health-sunday/.

[42] Julie Nichols, "Neurodiversity and LGBTQ Identity Can Intersect. Is Your Parish Supporting Us?" January 17, 2024, https://uscatholic.org/articles/202401/neurodiversity-and-lgbtq-identity-can-intersect-is-your-parish-supporting-us/.

[43] "LGBTQ+" NHS Dorset Neurodiversity Hub, https://nhsdorset.nhs.uk/neurodiversity/living/lgbtq/, accessed September 30, 2024.

[44] John Anderson, "LGBTQIA+ and Neurodiversity: The Links Between Neurodivergence and Being LGBTQ+," The Brain Charity, https://www.thebraincharity.org.uk/lgbtqia-neurodiversity-neurodivergent-lgbtq/, accessed September 30, 2024.

[45] Nick Walker, *Neuroqueer Heresies: Notes on the Neurodiversity Paradigm, Autistic Empowerment, and Postnormal Possibilities* (Autonomous Press, 2021).

[46] Walker, "Neuroqueer Heresies," 37.

[47] Walker, "Neuroqueer Heresies," 54.

[48] Walker, "Neuroqueer Heresies," 162–63.

[49] Alicia T. Crosby, "A Prayer for Those Refusing to Hide," Facebook video, August 25, 2024, https://www.facebook.com/aliciatcrosby/videos/here-is-a-prayer-for-those-refusing-to-hideholy-onegive-us-what-we-need-to-befor/780509060696794/?mibextid=WC7FNe&rdid=m4gBylFci0dYiRj1

Chapter Eight

[50] "Neurodiverse Worship at St. George's," St. George's Episcopal Church, accessed September 30, 2024, https://ndworship.org/.

[51] "Accessibility and Neurodiversity," Abiding Presence Lutheran Church, accessed September, 30, 2024, https://abidingpresence.net/accessibility-neurodiversity.

[52] "Accessibility and Neurodiversity," Abiding Presence Lutheran Church, accessed September, 30, 2024, https://abidingpresence.net/accessibility-neurodiversity.

[53] Katherine Martinelli, "Neurodivergent Kids and Screen Time: Embracing the Benefits While Building a Balance," Child Mind Institute, childmind.org/article/screens-and-neurodivergent-kids/.

[54] Samara Cole Doyon, *Next Level: A Hymn in Gratitude for Neurodiversity* (Ann Arbor, MI: Tilbury House Publishers, 2024).

[55] "We Do Kindness Around Mental Illness and Mental Health, and We Celebrate Neurodiversity," Galileo Christian Church, accessed September 30, 2024, https://www.galileochurch.org/we-do-kindness.

[56] Rev. Jess Harren, "How to Welcome Those with Disabilities in Church, Lower Susquehanna Synod, accessed September 30, 2024, https://www.lss-elca.org/how-to-welcome-those-with-disabilities-in-church/.

[57] "Neurodiversity and the Church: Essays on Neurodiverse Theology and Ministry," The Theology & Neurodiversity Project, accessed September 30, 2024, https://www.theologyandneurodiversity.com/essays/neurodiversity-and-the-church.

[58] United Church of Christ Mental Health Network, accessed October 25, 2024, https://www.mhn-ucc.org/.

[59] Richard Boswell, "Neurodiversity, Inclusive Pedagogy and the Need for Peer Support in Postsecondary Education," January 2020, https://www.researchgate.net/publication/352135876_Neurodiversity_Inclusive_Pedagogy_and_the_Need_for_Peer_Support_in_Postsecondary_Education_Neurodiversity_Inclusive_Pedagogy_and_the_Need_for_Peer_Support_in_Postsecondary_Education.

[60] First Congregational United Church of Christ of Indianapolis, Indiana Youth Group Covenant, November 2023.

Chapter Nine

[61] Mya Jaradat, "Religious Leaders Struggle with Burnout, Depression and Anxiety—Just Like the Rest of America," *Deseret News*, May 11, 2022, https://www.deseret.com/faith/2022/5/11/23058739/religious-leaders-struggle-with-burnout-depression-and-anxiety-pastor-mental-health-worker-shortage/.

[62] Lamar Hardwick, *Disability and the Church: A Vision for Diversity and Inclusion* (Downers Grove, IL: Intervarsity Press, 2021).

[63] Hardwick, *Disability and the Church*, 127.

[64] Lamar Hardwick, *How Ableism Fuels Racism: Dismantling the Hierarchy of Bodies in the Church* (Brazos Press, February 2024).

[65] Hardwick, *Disability and the Church*, 89.

[66] Hardwick, *Disability and the Church*, 71.

[67] Hardwick, *Disability and the Church*, 90.

[68] Hardwick, *Disability and the Church*, 3.

[69] Hardwick, *Disability and the Church*, 173.

[70] Hardwick, *Disability and the Church*, 96–97.

[71] Kay Rohloff, "Your ADHD Pastor and You," Spark House blog, December 19, 2019, https://blog.wearesparkhouse.org/your-adhd-pastor-and-you.

[72] "Making Progress in Engaging with Neurodiversity," Diocese of Winchester, February 4, 2024, https://winchester.anglican.org/making-progress-in-engaging-with-neurodiversity/.

[73] Emily Hammond, "NeuroWild Shift" Facebook post, October 22, 2024, https://www.facebook.com/people/NeuroWild/100087870753308/?mibextid=LQQJ4d&rdid=wLV0HaZeHOeVtzOl&share_url=https%3A%2F%2Fwww.facebook.com%2Fshare%2F1ZWpVqjeMD%2F%3Fmibextid%3DLQQJ4d.

[74] Emily Hammond, personal communication to the author, October 12, 2024

[75] Emily Hammond, personal communication to the author, September 3, 2024

[76] Emily Hammond, personal communication to the author, August 21, 2024

Chapter Ten

[77] Leah Lakshmi Piepzna-Samarasinha, *The Future is Disabled: Prophecies, Love Notes, and Mourning Songs* (Vancouver: Arsenal Pulp Press, 2022).

[78] Lisa Miller, *The Awakened Brain: The New Science of Spirituality and our Quest for an Inspired Life* (New York: Random House, 2021).

[79] Christine Valters Painter, *Birthing the Holy: Wisdom from Mary to Nurture Creativity and Renewal* (South Bend, IN: Ave Maria Press, 2022).

[80] E. Raffety and M. Insa-Iglesias, "Re-Imagining Christian Education through Neurodivergent Fellowship, Play, and Leadership in Online Videogaming," *Gamevironments*19 (2023): 80–114. Available at https://journals.suub.uni-bremen.de/.

[81] Raffety and Insa-Iglesias, "Re-imagining."

[82] Steven Naifeh and Gregory White Smith, *Van Gogh: The Life* (New York: Random House, 2011), 4.

[83] Naifeh and Smith *Van Gogh*, 202.

[84] Naifeh and Smith, *Van Gogh*, 207.

Glossary

[85] Leah Smith, "#Ableism," Center for Disability Rights blog, accessed September 30, 2024, https://cdrnys.org/blog/uncategorized/ableism/.

[86] "Understanding the Definition of Accessibility," Equity & Access, accessed September 30, 2024, https://www.ace-ed.org/understanding-the-definition-of-accessibility/.

[87] John Marble, Khushboo Chabria, and Ranga Jayaraman, *Neurodiversity for Dummies* (Hoboken, NJ: Wiley, 2024), 24.

[88] "Diversity and Inclusion Definitions," Ferris State University, accessed September 30, 2024, https://www.ferris.edu/administration/president/DiversityOffice/Definitions.htm.